AGAINST THE STREAM

The Adoption of Traditional Christian Faiths by Young Adults

Richard P. Cimino

Religion Watch
and
University Press of America, Inc.
Lanham • New York • London

Copyright © 1997 by
University Press of America, ® Inc.
4720 Boston Way
Lanham, Maryland 20706

3 Henrietta Street
London, WC2E 8LU England

Library of Congress Cataloging-in-Publication Data

Cimino, Richard P.
Against the stream : the adoption of traditional Christian faiths by
young adults / by Richard P. Cimino.
p.   cm.
Includes bibliographical references.
l. United States--Church history--20th century. 2. Conversion. 3.
Young adults--United States--Religious life. 4. Catholic church--
United States--Membership. 5. Reformed church--United States--
Membership. 6. Orthodox Eastern Church--United States--
Membership. I. Title.
BR526.C56 1996   277.3'0829'0842--dc20   96-35834 CIP

ISBN 0-7618-0574-5 (cloth: alk. ppr.)
ISBN 0-7618-0575-3 (pbk. : alk. ppr.)

⊖™The paper used in this publication meets the minimum
requirements of American National Standard for information
Sciences—Permanence of Paper for Printed Library Materials,
ANSI Z39.48—1984

For My Parents,
Stephen and Nancy

Table Of Contents

PREFACE

This book started out as project for the M.A. program in the Sociology of Religion at Fordham University. While the original project was based on interviews with Catholic and Reformed young adults, I enlarged the study to include Eastern Orthodox subjects after my graduation in 1994. I wish to thank my advisor Michael Cuneo, who read early drafts of the manuscript and encouraged me to blend journalistic skills with sociological fieldwork and insights. I should add, however, that the hybrid nature of this book—existing somewhere between journalism and sociology—is my own doing. I would also like to thank James Kelly of Fordham's Sociology Department for his helpful comments on the manuscript. The same gratitude goes to my cousin Peter D'Agostino who provided a much needed historian's perspective on the Reformed and Catholic chapters of the manuscript. I also appreciate the comments and criticisms of anonymous reviewers from various publishers. Linda and Scott Diamond of Diamond Computing Associates provided me with their usual professional service in preparing this manuscript for publication.

Since this book is based on my interviews with 30 young adults, I would especially like to thank the clergy, church officials and other people who provided valuable information on the phenomenon of "young traditionalism" and then put me into contact with the interviewees. The concern to protect the anonymity of the young adults unfortunately prevents me from thanking these individuals by name. Finally, I thank the 30 young adults for taking the time to discuss their lives and beliefs with me.

INTRODUCTION

In researching and reporting on contemporary religion, I have been intrigued by two developments that appear to be taking place simultaneously. On one hand, there is a growing body of research suggesting that Americans in the baby boom and younger generations are alienated from traditional religious institutions and increasingly "picking and choosing" their beliefs and churches according to consumer tastes and preferences. It is not unusual to find congregations that have tailored their services to spiritual "seekers," such as by de-emphasizing traditional liturgy and featuring entertainment-oriented contemporary music and drama. On the other hand, there is the phenomenon of American young adults who are returning or converting to traditional faiths, often making significant life changes in the process.

Within Judaism, there have been several books and studies on young adult professionals who have traded their secular and individualistic lifestyles to become Orthodox Jews. There have also been news reports of young adults adopting traditional forms of Catholic, Protestant and Eastern Orthodox Christianity. Conservative Catholic lay and religious orders that stress obedience to the pope and the wearing of traditional habits are attracting young people while traditional liberal-oriented orders continue to decline. A steady stream of converts, often baby boomers and those younger, are entering into the once largely ethnic world of Eastern Orthodoxy. Small conservative Presbyterian bodies that emphasize a return to classic Calvinist confessions are growing and often drawing young people into pro-life activism, while liberal Presbyterian and other Reformed churches decline or languish.

In studying these two seemingly conflicting developments, I often wondered how different these "traditional" young adults actually are from their counterparts who have dropped out of churches and synagogues altogether or who have taken to the spiritual marketplace. Is there any connection between these journeys into traditional religion and the more individualistic and consumeristic patterns of faith? Such concerns are often related to larger questions about how such an adoption of all-embracing religious traditions is possible in a society where pluralism, secularism and other stresses of modernity tend to destabilize faiths and worldviews that seek a continuity with the past. I realized that the only way to find answers to these questions was to track down some of these young adult traditional Christians and talk with them about their conversions and returns to traditional religiosity. This book is the result of such interviews with 30 young adults involved in Catholic, Reformed (or Calvinist), and Eastern Orthodox groups. In interviewing these "young traditionalists," I was as much interested in how their faith affected their lifestyles and social attitudes as in their beliefs. I wanted to find out how these young adults adhered to demanding faiths that seek to direct the contours of their whole lives while living in a modern society that often makes very different demands upon them.

Who Are The Young Traditionalists?

There is no doubt that young adults holding to traditional faiths make up a minority and are, in the words of one Catholic I interviewed, "going against the stream" both within their generation and within American religious life itself. Most studies and polls have continuously shown a decline in traditional religiosity among young people in terms of church attendance and full adherence to church teachings. In a major study of baby boomer religion, sociologist Wade Clark Roof found that as children the baby boomer generation were as religiously active as any generation before them. But by their early 20s, slightly more than one-fourth were involved to the same extent; the great majority had dropped out altogether. The high dropout rate did not mean that a large portion of baby boomers became atheists or agnostics—only a small minority did. Rather, the baby boomers adopted more consumeristic and individualistic forms of religiosity. For instance, far more respondents (53 percent) in Roof's survey view "being alone and meditating" as an important activity compared to that of "worshipping with others" (29 percent). [1]

Even when baby boomers have returned to institutional religious faith, many of them tend to value congregations for the services they provide, such as day care and Sunday school for their children, or relevant and practical preaching, rather than for fostering specific denominational or theological identities.[2] A similar alienation from religious institutions and tendency toward selective spirituality is reported to be evident among those in the younger generation known as the baby busters or "generation X." [3]

If young adults adhering to traditional religiosity are a minority, this does not mean that they are insignificant. When young adults return to regular religious practice, they tend to gravitate more to conservative than to liberal mainline Protestant congregations. Roof shows that the younger segment of the baby boom generation (those born between 1955 and 1962) are less alienated from religious institutions and more traditional in their lifestyles and religious preferences than older baby boomers[4]. It has also been shown that religious differences, such as between liberals and conservatives, are not so much between older and younger generations as within age groups. In a survey of 113,000 people asked about their religious affiliation, City University of New York researchers Barry Kosmin and Seymour Lachman found little evidence for a generation gap based on religious identity.

> The data on the diversity of religious opinion and the religious marketplace show that every age group is highly segmented...Rather than being a generational battle, the culture war over gender and family issues involves a clash of values that divides within generations. It pits believers in personal autonomy and right-based individualism against communitarians and traditionalists who advocate the common good and take issue with the unencumbered sovereignty of the individual. [5]

Gilles Kepel, a French scholar of religious movements, found that one of the common characteristics behind the conservative religious "revival" movements in Islam, European Catholicism and American Protestantism is that they attract a large base of university-trained, professional young adults.[6] A recent survey by Democratic pollster

Peter Hart found that young adults are more sympathetic to religious right politicians than older groups of Americans. The poll asked people whether they would be more or less likely to support a candidate if they learned he "was closely associated with right-wing religious groups and supported the positions of the religious right." Among older age groups the "right-wing" religious label generated more negative than positive feelings. But those in the 18-29 age group actually said they would be more likely to support such a candidate. Such a finding confirms previous research showing that among evangelicals, the young are about 20 percentage points likelier than the old to support the Republican Party.[7]

It should be noted that the young traditionalists are different from the many young adults who have converted to evangelical and fundamentalist churches even though they may share conservative religious and social views. Many evangelical churches today put little emphasis on denominational identity nor do they seek to return to a definable, historic religious tradition (although it is obvious that evangelicalism and fundamentalism are both traditions in a historical and sociological sense). In the burgeoning charismatic and Pentecostal churches, for instance, one finds little mention of adhering to classical confessional creeds or seeking roots in history, except in recovering or reexperiencing New Testament Christianity. In such churches there is much more of an emphasis on present day experience, such as being born again or being led by the Holy Spirit to individual interpretations of the Bible. The young traditionalists also differ from fundamentalists (such as independent and many Southern Baptists) who seek to return to the basics or "fundamentals" of biblical Christianity rather than to a comprehensive historical tradition. Other conservative Protestant churches, however, put a much greater emphasis on tradition and the role of creeds and confessions in forming a Christian identity, such as conservative Anglican, Lutheran and Reformed bodies. Such Protestants are similar to conservative Catholics and Eastern Orthodox believers in that they intentionally seek to recover a faith system from the past, as embodied in century-old confessions, theologies, church teachings, writings from the church fathers and various spiritual disciplines, and apply it to the present.

Some readers may wonder why I chose the Reformed, Catholic and Eastern Orthodox traditions when there are many other movements seeking to revitalize and retrieve traditional religion in other churches.

Why is the book focused exclusively on religiously and often socially conservative young adults as representing the Christian turn to tradition? Without a doubt, there are young adults converting to Mennonite, Quaker and Catholic groups who are seeking to recover more radical traditions based around pacifism and the communal lifestyle of the Anabaptists and the early church. There are also moderate Presbyterians who would sharply distinguish the views of the subjects from their own conception of the Reformed tradition. It should be noted, however, that the churches and groups from which I interviewed the young adults are highly visible and influential in the American Christian community and show steady signs of growth, even though there has been little research on them. These groups can also serve as a test case of the phenomenon of young adults seeking to retrieve traditional faiths within the three major Christian groupings—Catholic, Protestant, and Eastern Orthodox. Although these young traditionalists are far from making up a unified movement, they are in closer contact with each other than has been the case with previous generations of such believers. For instance, the new journal *Regeneration Quarterly* has attracted a large readership of conservative Christian younger baby boomers and busters—with strong Catholic, Reformed and Orthodox participation—for dialogue on a wide range of social and theological issues.

Because this phenomenon of traditional Christian young adults is mostly uncharted territory for researchers, this book is exploratory in nature. I did not approach this study with a set of sociological theories or a conceptual framework in which to fit the subjects' views. The fact that these churches and movements, which are often portrayed as too demanding or even outmoded for modern society, are attracting young adults seemed reason enough to study them. If I did approach these movements with any preconceived theories it would be with the unremarkable view that their success in drawing young adults shows that they are meeting needs created by modern society.

In doing some preliminary reading on this subject, I was impressed with research by sociologist Lynn Davidman on a movement of young women who had converted to Orthodox Jewish groups. An outside observer might think that these Orthodox initiates, who often had careers and independent lifestyles, were largely concerned with finding a religious faith and spirituality. Through participant observation, however, Davidman found that such groups were valued because they provided members with clearly defined gender roles in a changing society rather than a spiritual experience (some of Davidman's subjects were not even sure of the existence of God). The Orthodox Jewish groups gave high status to marriage and motherhood (as well as supportive male roles within marriage), something that these women did not find in secular society.[8]

Davidman's work led me to the view that the different religious groups I planned to study may serve to solve for their adherents different problems and needs created by modern society. Such an approach would focus not so much on how these movements impact their members' lives but would instead examine what the members themselves take from these groups to fulfill their own social and religious needs. I found that the different traditions did provide the subjects with different tools for confronting the central dilemmas of modernity, such as pluralism, privatization, and individualism. In fact, the subjects often selected and reinterpreted certain parts of their traditions in order to help them solve such problems.

About The Interviews

This book focuses on 30 young adults between the ages of 23 to 35 years old who have either converted or returned to traditional or conservative Catholicism, the Reformed faith, and Eastern Orthodoxy. Ten young adults were interviewed from within each group. Since there have been no surveys of young participants in these groups, it is impossible to prove whether or not the 30 young traditionalists represent the "typical" conservative or traditional Roman Catholic, Reformed or Eastern Orthodox Christian. While the sample of subjects cannot be said to be statistically representative of young adults in these traditions, the case studies do appear to illuminate significant dimensions of this conversion and return phenomenon. I selected most of the young adults from a list of referrals provided by leaders, fellow members and others associated with these groups. The groups from which I selected most of the young traditionalists represent many of the views and concerns found in the wider Catholic, Reformed and Eastern Orthodox bodies. In my interviews I also found that the subjects' beliefs were similar to those found in literature published by organizations that are often said to represent the young traditionalists in these church bodies.

I was not concerned, however, to interview the most "religiously correct" subjects whose views were closely aligned with their leaders and churches. In order to avoid interviewing only members of one tightly-knit group with strongly uniform views, I tried to speak with people from at least two different groups from within each tradition. For instance, I selected Reformed young adults from three different churches and denominations. I also decided not to focus on the structures, activities and leaderships of the young traditionalists' churches and fellowship groups (I did not confer with clergy on either the interview questions or the subjects' responses), although I did attend services of the churches in which at least some of them were members. The purpose of the study was not to examine the inner-workings of these young adults' churches nor the processes by which they were initiated and socialized into their faiths (all important subjects which could make books in their own right), but rather to find out how these young traditionalists understand and apply their faith to everyday life. In other words, I was more interested in the young adults' accounts and "versions" of their faith rather than in the official interpretations of their belief and behavior provided by their respective churches. While these young traditionalist no doubt seek to follow all the teachings of their churches, their interpretations and applications of these traditions were often quite different (especially among the Catholics and Eastern Orthodox), even among those within the same churches.

I selected the age range of 23-35 (which means, in the time frame of my interviews, that they were born between 1958 and 1970) for the study because it covers the younger cohort of baby boomers as well as the baby buster or "twentysomething" generation. As noted above, researchers have shown that the younger baby boomers and baby busters take a more conservative approach to social issues and religion than the older baby boomers, yet they are also affected by the same consumerist and choice-based currents as their older siblings. Young adults in this age range are in the process of developing independent lives, finding careers, and forming families. They are at a period in their lives when they are highly influenced by the social currents of the times and are searching for moral norms and a faith by which to live. It is also the case that the three traditions under study in this book have attracted a significant number of leaders and members who are baby boomers and younger. The fact that all of the young traditionalists lived during the time of their interviews in the New

York metropolitan area might make my sample less than typical of other cases of young adult conversion to traditional Christian groups. The New York area, especially Manhattan, has been uniquely influenced by modernity and pluralism. In fact, since my study focuses on how young adults relate their faith to modern society, the New York context serves as an excellent laboratory in this respect. It should be noted, however, that only about one-quarter of the young adults worked or lived in Manhattan; most of them lived in the more "traditional" outer boroughs and suburbs.

Each subject was asked open-ended questions relating to: religious background prior to involvement in traditional religiosity; accounts of conversions or returnings; the extent and patterns of their religious commitment; attitudes over issues of family life, sexuality and other areas of cultural conflict with traditional religions; attitudes toward other faiths; involvement, interest, and attitudes on political and social issues; conflicts and problems that have emerged over the young adults' adopted faiths; and attitudes toward change and liberalization within their faiths. The length of the interviews ranged from approximately one hour to three hours. The interviews were usually conducted in the young adults' homes, places of business or a public meeting place, such as a diner (when possible, I tried not to interview subjects in churches in order to insure for greater candor). All of the young traditionalists' names are pseudonyms and other details of their lives that might jeopardize their anonymity have also been changed. Aside from such changes, I have attempted to cite and quote their words and views as they were related to me in the interviews.

This book is organized around accounts of my interviews with these young adults. Integrated within the chapters of these narratives are overviews of the movements and trends relating to young adult religiosity within each religious tradition, as well as analyses of the patterns of beliefs, practices and attitudes evident among the young traditionalists. Such analyses also include an examination of pertinent literature that may shed light on the phenomenon of young adult involvement in these faith traditions. The book concludes with a comparison of the three traditions and a discussion about what such young adult conversions and returns to faith may reveal about the relation of traditional religion to modernity and, more specifically, religious consumerism. Throughout this study I have attempted to be as objective and unbiased as possible and to refrain from evaluating and judging the truth claims of the three traditions. If it is impossible to attain complete objectivity, I hope I have fully exercised the ideal of fairness in these pages.

CHAPTER 1:
The Roman Catholic Tradition

Anyone who watched television during the visit of Pope John Paul II to Denver in August, 1993 was familiar with the polls newscasters ran showing a high rate of dissent among American Catholics. The younger generations especially dissented on a wide number of church positions, including the prohibitions against artificial birth control, sex outside marriage, remarriage after divorce, married priests and the ordination of women to the priesthood. Yet it must have seemed strange to some viewers that these statistics were often juxtaposed with film clips of multitudes of enthusiastic young people cheering on an elderly pope who is the embodiment of such teachings—a scenario that has been repeated the world over. Such fleeting images clashed with the popular view that there are almost two Catholic churches in America: one church led by the pope and other leaders consisting mainly of older traditional members, and the other made up of largely modern younger Americans who pay little heed to tradition or church authority as they pick-and-choose their own beliefs. It may be the case that many of these enthusiastic young people were attracted more by the camaraderie of the crowds and the charismatic presence of a famous figure than by the Catholic faith. Yet the large turnout in Denver and the reported enthusiasm and claims of renewed faith in parishes around the country in the wake of the papal visit does suggest that Catholicism is appealing to a segment of young people.

There is more truth than falsehood in the claim that most young adults brought up Catholic are far from being traditional or observant in their faith. Since the Second Vatican Council, there has been growing dissent against many official church teachings, and it is often

1

those in the baby boomer and buster generations who are the least observant of their faith and the most questioning of authority. Wade Clark Roof's research on the baby boomers finds that while the Catholic Church has retained more of its members than the Protestants—81 percent of those baby boomers who grew up Catholic still identify with the faith—two-thirds of Catholic boomers who dropped out of the church while growing up still don't show up for Mass. Other findings show a similar pattern: 85 percent of Catholic baby boomers say that going to church every Sunday is not necessary to be a good Catholic; 81 percent do not subscribe to church teachings on divorce and remarriage, and 68 percent in this age group disagrees with its position on abortion.[1] The same level of dissent is evident among younger Catholics, especially on sexual issues, as they place a greater emphasis on selecting beliefs rather than holding to a more comprehensive faith. In studying former Catholic high school students (who would be in the age-range of the subjects interviewed in this study), sociologist Patrick McNamara found that since graduating, less than half attend a parish regularly, and they are "liberal" on most sexual issues, except abortion. These students emphasized the primacy of following their conscience rather than church teachings in making life decisions.[2]

Yet there are signs that those young Catholics who have found their way to regular religious practice are taking a more conservative approach to the faith. A recent study of Catholic students at a secular university found that those who regularly attended Mass were significantly more likely to accept church teachings on abortion and sexuality than those attending occasionally.[3] A nationwide survey of American Catholics by Purdue University found that baby boomer Catholics were more likely than baby busters to score low on an index of Catholic beliefs and practices, such as belief in the Virgin Mary as the mother of God and that the Catholic Church represents the true faith. While the baby busters and baby boomers were similar in their liberal attitudes on women's ordination and sexual issues, the more conservative views on doctrine among the younger age group confirms anecdotal information the researchers gathered from some church leaders who see a "rebound" effect in the younger generation. Such church leaders are finding a "significant number of young people who are embracing traditional beliefs and practices...perhaps longing for an anchor of tradition that they see as having been rejected by their parents."[4]

The current generation of Catholic seminarians and priests are reported to be more conservative in doctrine than preceding generations. A study in 1993 by sociologist Dean Hoge found that the youngest priests (ages 26-35) are far more conservative than their predecessors on several issues. These young priests have more in common with older priests (over 60) than with the age cohort in between (roughly those in the range of the early baby boom). For instance, in 1970, 85 percent of priests age 26-35 supported optional celibacy; today only 45 percent of young priests do.[5] A spate of new conservative and traditional Catholic publications have been founded in the last decade often with strong support and leadership from young adults, including *Catholic World Report, Inside the Vatican, New Oxford Review,* and the *Latin Mass.*[6] Most of the Catholic religious orders which have recently been reconstituted or founded, such as the Franciscan Sisters of Renewal and Monks of the Holy Cross, are strongly conservative and are attracting an impressive number of young people as compared to the declining established liberal orders. These orders stress obedience to Rome and the wearing of traditional habits.[7] Older conservative orders such Opus Dei are also growing among young Catholic religious and laity. In one study, it was recently found that more tradition-oriented orders for Catholic women are twice as likely to draw young recruits than the less conservative groups.[8] There is also a growing conservative youth movement expressed in such groups as Youth 2000. This nationwide effort, started in 1993 (after the pope's visit), draws youth from the ages of 15 to 30 to crowded retreats where participants pray the rosary, mediate on the Eucharist and listen to preaching provided by the conservative Franciscan Friars of the Renewal.

There are no statistics available on the number of young conservative Catholics. In reviewing survey research, sociologist Andrew Greeley found that the number of conservative Catholics is dwindling and that they are more likely to be elderly and have a propensity to racism and sexism.[9] Greeley's study drew a good amount of fire from conservatives and other critics who protested that he examined only a small minority of reactionary conservatives in his analysis. While Greeley is correct in saying that the majority of young people calling themselves Catholics are neither traditional nor conservative, the research cited above indicates that there are a significant number of such Catholics among those converting to the church and returning to regular practice. Even if they are a minority in the church, such active conservative believers are more likely to make an impact on Catholicism in the coming years than the many who have loose ties to the institution.

The trend of young adults converting or returning to more traditional forms of Catholicism did not emerge in a vacuum. These young people inhabit an American Catholic landscape marked by fissures and faultlines over matters of doctrine and practice. While there has always been battles between liberals and conservatives or traditionalists in Catholicism, the polarization between different segments of the church grew after the Second Vatican Council. The council sought to update the Catholic church's teachings and practices to meet the challenges of the modern world through such measures as giving laity a greater role in church and society, permitting Masses to be said in the vernacular, and supporting dialogue and cooperation with secular society and with other religions. As many changes introduced at Vatican II began to be implemented in dioceses and parishes, especially in Europe and North America, many Catholics began to protest that such reforms were being carried too far. Such conservative Catholics claimed that the documents of Vatican II were misinterpreted by liberals who sought to accommodate the church according to secular ideologies and thereby empty the Catholic tradition of much of its supernatural and comprehensive authority. Conservatives maintain that the Vatican II documents attempted to conserve Catholic truth while giving laypeople a greater role in the church and the world to carry out such teachings. This group of Catholics, according to sociologist Michael Cuneo, believes that the

> church's doctrinal and ethical certitudes, luxuriant ritualism, imperial government, and supernaturalist ethos has been successively downgraded. These elements had served for many Catholics as the signposts of a religious culture that was a sacred realissimum, an eternal citadel protected against the contigencies of human meanings and social change...But this enchanted canopy has been sundered, as pluralism, a mitigated situation ethics, and a catechizes which invokes the primacy of experience as its point of departure have become the common backdrop—in the pew,

confessional, and seminary—for the daily performance of Catholic life. [10]

As liberal groups increasingly began to press for such issues as women's ordination, increased lay leadership in the church and openness to non-Catholic theological currents during the late 1960s and 70s, conservative Catholics responded by creating organizations to counteract these initiatives (for example, the conservative Women for Faith and Family was created to undercut the influence of feminism in the church, and the Fellowship of Catholic Scholars was formed to challenge liberalism in Catholic academia, such as in the Catholic Theological Society.) Often there is a strong political and social dimension to conservative Catholicism, supporting such causes as pro-life activism, school choice for parents, and protesting increasing secularism and anti-Catholicism in society. Although there are notable exceptions (such as Catholics represented by New Oxford Review magazine), conservative Catholics often support politically conservative measures, such as free market economics and strong defense policies.

Under Pope John Paul II, the conservatives have steadily gained more influence in the American church. Conservative bishops, such as John Cardinal O'Connor of New York and Archbishop Francis Stafford of Denver, have been chosen to lead influential dioceses. A newly Vatican-issued universal catechism has been hailed by conservatives as serving a bulwark against liberal theological influence in the church. The movement has attracted prominent converts—often from mainline and evangelical Protestantism—who have become spokesman for the cause, including such intellectuals as Thomas Howard, George Rutler, Richard John Neuhaus, Scott Hahn, Paul and Evelyn Vitz, Sheldon Vanauken and Dale Vree. Such alleged Marian apparitions as those in Medjugorje in the former Yugoslavia and the Catholic charismatic movement have both been instrumental in moving many Catholics to a more conservative form of the faith. The Franciscan University in Steubenville, Ohio, has moved from being strictly a center of charismatic Catholic activity (such as in promoting healings and speaking in tongues) to emphasizing conservative themes while still maintaining a unique evangelistic thrust. In the last 15 years conservative Catholic publications, publishing houses, schools and organizations have mushroomed. Although still a minority within

American Catholicism, conservatives have created a durable and influential subculture based around loyalty to the pope, especially Pope John Paul II, and a recovery of Catholic cultural influence and traditional practices.

But for some Catholics, the conservatives have not gone far enough. Shortly after Vatican II, a movement of Catholics emerged that rejected much of Vatican II, believing that it was a heretical attempt by church liberals in order to turn aside centuries of Catholic tradition. The rallying point for these "traditionalist" Catholics is the pre-Vatican II (or Tridentine) Latin Mass rather than the New Rite Mass in the vernacular introduced shortly after the council. Following such leaders as the late Archbishop Marcel Lefebvre (who was excommunicated for his stand), strict Catholic traditionalists make a wholesale indictment on the modern church: they claim its liturgy is unCatholic and that it has abandoned Catholic culture and civilization for the false gods of democracy and pluralism (most traditionalists oppose the separation of church and state, calling for the establishment of a Catholic state).[11]

Much of the traditionalist movement is found in separatist groups, such as the Society of St. Pius X founded by Lefebvre or the numerous independent chapels around the country. But many other traditionalists have remained in the conciliar church, attending the Latin Masses now permitted in many dioceses. In recent years, there is reported to be a growing interest in the Latin Mass among young adults—a generation that has no recollection of pre-Vatican II days. Charles Coulombe, a young Catholic traditionalist speaker and writer, estimates that as much as 40 to 70 percent of his audiences at his lectures are younger than 35 years old. Coulombe said that many of these new traditionalists are converts or are lapsed Catholics who were formerly involved in anything from Protestant fundamentalism to the New Age movement. He believes that the "sense of the mystical," expressed in the Latin Mass and the Catholic contemplative tradition, is often what draws these newcomers.[12] Roger McCaffery, the publisher of the *Latin Mass* magazine (and himself a baby boomer), finds that the "enthusiasm of the post-Vatican II generation is equal to the enthusiasm of the pre-Vatican II people" about the Latin Mass.[13]

Conservatives and traditionalists (and scholars studying these two movements) may not appreciate the fact that the two groups are placed together in this study. While there are significant differences (and hostilities) between these groups, they do share the common experience of seeking to retrieve the Catholic tradition. This study will at least show that such acts of retrieval mean different things to different Catholics. It is important to note that the divisions between traditionalists and conservatives are not as deep and laden with emotion among younger Catholics as they are among older ones. It is not at all unusual to find young people somewhere between the conservative and traditionalist camps; for instance, they would be devoted to the Latin Mass, while accepting the documents of Vatican II (a group which represents several of the young adults that I interviewed). In order to maintain some uniformity in referring to the Catholic Church, it should be noted that all of the young adults attending the Latin Mass do not belong to separatist groups, but instead attend parishes where the Latin rite is permitted by the local diocese. Readers should be reminded that this study is not so much about the doctrinal fine points (such as interpretations of the Second Vatican Council) among Catholics as much as about how their faith affects their lifestyles and attitudes. The young adults interviewed were chosen from among a parish which serves the Latin Mass, a conservative Franciscan order for the laity, and through referrals from other subjects.

Discovering And Recovering The Faith

Elizabeth Phelan lived in a housing project in a rundown section of the Bronx. In entering her apartment from the dilapidated hallway, I felt as if I had walked into a monastery. The living room was sparsely furnished and the walls were lined with crucifixes and colorful icons of saints and the Virgin Mary. Religious statues and candles crowded the bookshelves. Phelan was an attractive woman of 26 who wore a long plain dress and rosary beads with a large wooden cross around her wrist. She and the two conservative Catholic young women with whom she lived were members of a new conservative lay Franciscan order. Aside from her work as an accountant, Phelan often worked with the children in the project. I asked whether she and her roommates saw themselves as engaged in a mission to the project and neighborhood. "We're more on a mission to ourselves," she answered somewhat cryptically. As I began speaking with other Catholic young adults, those words often came back to me and took on a greater semblance of meaning. They often spoke of claiming a Catholic identity through a good deal of individual searching and initiative. Their emphasis was not so much on transforming the world or even the church but on changing themselves.

Phelan said her journey to orthodox Catholicism took place when she was 24 and traveling on a plane to visit her parents during the Christmas holidays. The thought came to Phelan that if she died in a plane crash she might go to hell. She resolved to start following the church's teachings. After Phelan later heard talks by those involved in the reported apparitions of the Virgin Mary at Medjugorje, she started to say the Rosary and was drawn into a network of orthodox Catholic young people. Phelan was a practicing Catholic prior to her adoption of a more traditional faith. "I went to church every Sunday but partied on weekends. I never left the church physically but left it mentally as far as following church teachings," she said. She also came to the realization that she was in "mortal sin" by regularly receiving communion while she was having sexual relations with her boyfriend.[14]

Most of the other Catholic young adults I subsequently interviewed told stories similar to Phelan's. Mary Hensel, a 23-year-old artist and writer who is also a member of the Franciscan lay order, attended parochial school and was brought up in a charismatic Catholic home where traditional Catholic practices and teachings were downplayed. In college she experienced a long period of depression and began to feel that the Catholic church lacked a vital spirituality and was "dead." She had many evangelical Protestant friends and was considering joining one of their churches. But then she took a course in Catholic theology and "something happened." She read such "orthodox" writers and theologians as T.S. Eliot, G.K. Chesterton and Henri du Lubac and found herself fascinated with the "beauty of Catholicism. It was really my introduction to the church."[15]

James Ryan, a 31 year-old reporter with a financial newspaper in New Jersey, grew up in the 1970s believing that many church teachings could be viewed as "metaphors" rather than actual truth. But then he started doubting the validity of the theory of evolution, the first step which led to a more traditional faith. Ryan was studying in Ireland when he came across Medieval English literature. In such works he discovered the "richness of the church and the liturgy...I was never exposed to that in parochial school. I was never presented with the central thesis of Christianity and how it was so instrumental in the growth of civilization."[16]

What first struck me about these and other accounts of return among Catholic young adults was the sense of discovery they conveyed. Although most of the young adults I interviewed grew up Catholic, with several attending parochial schools, their journey into more traditional forms of the faith represented something of a conversion, not unlike accounts of born-again Christians who often speak of moving from the darkness of their sinful past into the light of salvation. Many subjects spoke of a time when they accepted the "liberal" views they were taught, but then found the truth. Phelan said of her religious upbringing, "In catechism we just learned that God is love....I didn't grow up hearing about sin. There was nothing on the saints or Mary. I feel sad for my own generation."

John Cuvic, a 28-year-old editor of a business magazine in New York, said he learned "virtually nothing" of Catholic teaching from 12 years of parochial school. He said he learned more about Catholicism through reading books his more traditional Catholic parents owned. He said in catechism class his teacher tried to turn students into "radical Catholics," through teaching on liberation theology and other contemporary theological currents. "The basic sentiment was that traditional church teachings were outdated and that the pope was out of touch with the modern world," he said. A priest told Cuvic that confession was not necessary for young people because they were not old enough to commit serious sins. At first, Cuvic found himself in agreement with such liberal teachings, but he became increasingly troubled by teachers whom he viewed as denying cardinal Catholic tenets, such as transubstantiation—the belief that the bread and wine in communion miraculously become the body and blood of Christ. He said he remembers thinking at one point that "these people [his teachers] are not new and exciting, they are evil." Cuvic added that this incident was an "emotional experience" that served as the turning point in his becoming involved in conservative and later traditionalist Catholicism. Of his turn to increasingly traditional forms of the faith, he said he was "awakening to information that was suppressed, ideas that were forgotten."[17]

The sense of searching for and discovering an obscure faith of which Cuvic spoke was more fully illustrated in the accounts of Michael Aubach and his wife Tara. Michael, a 35-year-old musician and graduate student, grew up in a strongly Catholic home in Pennsylvania and attended parochial schools until college. He was an altar boy and remembers helping serve the Mass when it was still said in Latin. Starting in the ninth grade he attended Mass only occasionally and became less interested in his faith, partly as a result of the changes taking place in the church and his Catholic school after Vatican II.

> It was like we were guinea pigs for certain new educational methods and theology programs...I remember one course called 'Personality and Vocational Development.' It took a strongly psychological approach and moved away from theology. There were also classes in Protestant theology and biblical criticism. There were all sorts of things that you never heard at home. It wasn't all bad; a lot of it was interesting. But it did damage because it was confusing. We were too young to take a lot of it in. It was a breakdown of authority. Who do you believe, the priest or your parents? A lot of people just gave up, saying, 'the heck with it all.'

Aubach did not become an atheist or agnostic, but instead sampled a wide variety of philosophies and spiritualities. "Whatever caught my fancy I took up for a month or so." He was especially interested in Eastern religions and Sufism [Islamic mystical teachings]. He dropped out of college to be a musician and lived a lifestyle that he said was "wild and hedonistic," with little sense of direction. When he was 29 he moved to New York and found a job at an occult bookstore. At the bookstore he became interested in an esoteric philosophy known as traditionalism. The philosophy teaches that all traditional faiths have a common mystical core of truth. Adopting this philosophy changed Aubach's outlook on life, giving him a respect for traditional religion, especially Catholicism. "I was able to look back at something worth preserving...I also started looking at [modern] Catholicism as a religion that was unraveling."

When Aubach attended a Latin Mass, he realized why he had always felt dissatisfied with the new rite or Novus Ordo Mass.

> In attending the new rite Mass, I felt like I was leaving one world and then entering the same world again. With the Latin Mass you go from one world into another world. There's something really

transcendent there. The New Rite is so banal, while [the Latin Mass] takes people out of themselves and the ordinary.

Aubach was considering joining one of the separatist traditionalist Catholic groups, but he felt a "rigidity" among the members that made him uncomfortable. He started attending a Latin Mass recently permitted by his local diocese. It was at this parish that he made a full return to Catholicism. When he heard a priest preaching that "we must all submit ourselves to God," he felt as if he was hit by a "thunderbolt...I realized how my pride kept me from submitting myself to God." After that he went to confession and became active in the parish. He still has questions about the "validity" of the new Mass and other recent innovations in the church, but added that he now finds himself "part of a community."[18]

Tara Aubach, a 30-year-old dancer, grew up in a New England home where there was almost a "complete rejection of organized religion." Her parents, both painters, had Unitarian and Congregationalist backgrounds but rarely went to church. Even as a young girl, however, she would visit friends' churches and "always had a desire for finding a religious path," often composing her own prayers and rituals before going to sleep at night. During her college years, she became a "basic heathen, dating and partying a lot, using drugs and drinking." After college she moved to New York and became interested in feminist spirituality, as well as reading widely in astrology and other New Age and alternative religions. During this time, she met a practicing Buddhist and became increasingly drawn to that faith. She was drawn to the most orthodox and traditional branch of the religion, Tibetan Buddhism. "I was always drawn to the purest expression of things, even in dance. I always wanted to find the source of things. Tibetan Buddhism had that purity. The faith was handed down from one generation to the next," she said. She moved into a Tibetan Buddhist center with Michael Aubach, who was then her boyfriend, even though he did not practice the faith.

While she was living in the Buddhist center, Tara began to have second thoughts about her newly adopted faith. On one occasion she found rosary beads Michael Aubach kept around the apartment and started praying the various rosary prayers. She was struck by the similarity of the rosary beads and her practice of using Buddhist meditation beads. When she went to Italy to be married, she found an "extremely powerful" attraction to the Catholic churches and shrines she visited. Aubach started regularly praying the Rosary and reading such Catholic writers as Thomas Merton and G.K. Chesterton. "I was beginning to feel more comfortable in Christianity. It was not as foreign as Buddhism. As hard as I tried, it was hard to escape the familiarity of Christianity in the culture." Back in New York, she started attending Masses but did not like what she saw.

> I came to Catholicism because I saw it as the source of Christianity. I didn't want something watered down. I would be all excited going out to Mass in the morning, and then I would return home almost paralyzed, saying to [Michael], 'Is this what Christ came up with? Is this it?' What I saw in modern Catholicism offended my sensibilities—the so-called music, the so-called art. It was worse than ugly. I felt that the Buddhist services had more authenticity

With her husband, she attended the services of a separatist traditionalist group, but did not like the idea that "they were separated from Rome." When she started going to the Latin Mass at a diocese parish, she finally felt at home. "I felt like something sacred was taking place. Even those who are repulsed by it feel that something is happening. The music, the art, the liturgy, everything comes together. The strong rituals that I found in Buddhism, I refound in Catholicism and the Latin Mass." Shortly after she started to attend the Latin Masses, Aubach was baptized and became a member of the parish. Along with attending the Latin Mass every week, she goes to daily Mass at a parish near her home in the New York City borough of Queens.[19]

Searching For The Church

The journey to more traditional forms of religiosity in the Catholic Church among the subjects took many paths. That should not be too surprising given the diversity of traditions and spiritualities in Catholicism. There is no one way of return or conversion to the Catholic tradition. In a way, the young adults mirror the pluralism that exists in the wider modern church. The subjects discovered or rediscovered the Catholic tradition often outside of institutional channels—in Medieval literature, unapproved Marian apparitions, new upstart religious orders, charismatic prayer meetings, the Tridentine Latin Mass, and pre-Vatican II Catholic and Anglo-Catholic writers and theologians. These different movements and subgroups have had little to do with each other. The more conservative Catholic members of the new Franciscan lay order had little attraction to the Latin Mass, while other subjects (both conservative and traditionalist) often criticized the Marian apparition movement and Catholic charismatics.

What is more surprising is the often individualistic and solitary routes and patterns of devotion taken by many of the subjects. While Catholicism has been considered a communal religion that seeks to bind together families and neighborhoods, the search for more traditional forms of the faith has taken these young Catholics in the direction of rebellion and non-conformity, often going against the wider church and society. For instance, John Cuvic soon became outspoken in his attacks on the liberal teachers at his parochial school. He attempted to get such teachers fired and alert parents to the school's liberal curriculum. "Instead of rebelling against my parents, like most teens do, I rebelled against my school." Cuvic, who said he was not popular among his peers, often sought out the advice of older priests to learn more about the traditional teachings of the church. While attending an ivy league university, Cuvic discovered Gregorian chant and other traditional forms of Catholic liturgy. He eventually gravitated toward going only to Latin Masses, believing the new Mass was a "betrayal" and "Protestant." Today Cuvic considers himself a traditionalist Catholic, although he does not belong to a separatist traditionalist group.

After Elizabeth Phelan resolved to adhere to church teachings, she attempted to go to confession but did not know how to go about it "since no one I knew went to confession." The young adult group in which Phelan became involved was an "orthodox" island in a largely liberal parish. She credits the strong support of new friends in the group for helping her remain strong in the faith. "Seeing people live out the faith and sometimes fall and make mistakes helped me feel more normal," Phelan said. Eventually she left the parish because of its "liberalism" and tolerance of dissent against Catholic teachings. Phelan credits her strong faith today also to her former boyfriend who, before he converted, used to question her about her new beliefs. "He was an atheist, so his questions and searching before he converted helped strengthen me as I thought things out for myself." Phelan viewed her experience of seeking and questioning as important. "A lot of people were forced to believe in my mother's generation. They had no choice. Today, my generation has to choose. We have to do searching in order to get faith. We're not just going to be lukewarm Christians."

The emphasis on choice and selecting one's beliefs and practices found among many young Catholics struck a responsive chord among the subjects, although in a somewhat different key. While seeking to adhere to a comprehensive tradition, the subjects find they also have to be selective to maintain their faith. They are very selective about which parish to attend, what Catholic school to send their children to, and from which priests they should seek confession and guidance. When James Ryan started attending Latin Masses (which were then not permitted by the church officials) after he arrived home from studying in Ireland, there were few role models or mentors who provided him with instruction or fellowship in his move toward a more traditional faith. He said that today he still finds his relationship with the organized church "kind of ill-defined." Today he frequently attends his local suburban parish for new rite Masses, while also making the long trip into New York on many Sundays to attend Latin Masses. "It's an inconvenience to have to seek out all these beautiful trappings in the church today," he said.

Michael and Tara Aubach have found a strong sense of community within the parish using the Latin Mass, but they are faced with dilemmas when they are out of town. When Michael Aubach is not able to attend a Latin Mass on Sundays, he usually tends to stays home. Tara Aubach attends new rite Masses, as well as Latin Masses, but prefers the latter. When her dance company goes on the road, she often has to make elaborate plans beforehand to attend a Latin Mass. "Sometimes when I call up some dioceses, they won't even tell me if they have any Latin Masses," she said, referring to many "liberal" Catholics' opposition to reinstating the Latin rite. When there is no other alternative, she attends Latin Masses offered by the schismatic traditionalist groups, such as the Society of St. Piux X. Both Michael and Tara Aubach view themselves as more socially and religiously moderate than many of the other parishioners at their parish. "There are those who are somewhat rigid in their thinking. Calling everyone heretics and becoming obsessed with homosexuality is not really what the faith is about. It doesn't help you spiritually," Tara said.

In some cases, priests and other clergy had a part to play in introducing subjects to a more traditional faith, although local parish priests did not often play this role. Phillip Halloran, a 26-year-old college student, was brought up in the Catholic Church but started to drift from the faith in high school. When he was 18 years old he heard a priest from out of town speak at his parish about the Marian apparitions at Medjugorge and was captivated, as much by the priest as the message. "I was blown away by this priest. I never saw anyone so holy. Something about him made me aware of the reality of God and Christ." Halloran went out of his way to arrange for the priest to hear his confession. "After confession, I felt an overwhelming peace. There were no worries, no inhibitions, just a sense of freedom and openness to other people." The priest became Halloran's spiritual director, even though he lived in another part of the country. Halloran also became involved in a conservative young adult fellowship and subsequently joined a new lay conservative Franciscan order. While he goes to Mass everyday, he is not strongly involved in his local parish. Most of his activities and friendships are based around the Franciscan lay group.[20]

The loose ties the subjects often had to parishes was evident in the account of Scott Eller, a 28-year-old stock broker. Eller converted to Christianity when he was 18 from a non-religious Jewish background. He spent about three years trying various evangelical churches before he decided he should put down roots in one tradition. Through the encouragement of charismatic Catholic friends and his own reading, he became convinced that Catholicism most fully taught the truth. "It's rooted in Christ and the apostles. I like the fact that it can be literally proven, that it can be traced back to Christ." He was considering becoming Eastern Orthodox, but the fact that the Catholics had the pope convinced him of the validity of the faith. Although Eller is strongly committed to Catholic teachings, he still has not found a parish home.

> I haven't found a parish where I feel I belong, where I'm comfortable. I usually go to two churches in the area, but I'm also looking for a good church where you get the feeling that there's a

lot of faith, where the priests are not watering down the faith...I'm
willing to travel a [moderate] distance to find a parish like that

He added that "a lot of parishes are dead," and that he sees it as his
responsibility to help bring to the church "renewal and more
community life." Although he is not as strongly identified with the
charismatic movement as he once was, he finds most of his fellowship
with his charismatic Catholic friends through informal gatherings,
prayer meetings, and occasional retreats.[21]

The Allure Of Rome

Why were these young adults attracted to conservative and
traditional Catholicism rather than to more liberal forms of the faith or
other religious groups? When sociologist Andrew Greeley was asked
why many Catholics stay in the church even though they disagree with
some of its teachings, he replied, "Because they like being Catholic."[22]
In a similar way, I wanted to find out about the appeal of this tradition
in a way that went beyond the intellectual reasons and rote answers the
subjects may have formulated. So I asked them what they liked most
and what they liked least about being Catholic. Elizabeth Phelan said
she likes the church's "never ending history and tradition. It's just not
boring. I love receiving the eucharist. I love hearing the truth. Society
a lot of times doesn't tell the truth—it's mainly concerned with
materialism as a way to be happy and feel good." Mary Hensel said
what she likes most about being Catholic is

> you get everything. There's nothing good in the world you can't
> have...You have access to every Christian tradition. You're really
> in a position of negotiation with the world. You have the truth and
> can't surrender it...But you are free to learn from the world and
> pick and choose what to accept.

The subjects who attended the Latin Masses were more likely than
the others to stress the mystical appeal of the Catholic traditions and
the liturgy. James Ryan said he is attracted to the

> beauty of traditional Catholicism, the rosary, the prayers, a lot of
> these things that have all this richness; that there are saints for
> every occasion, the devotion to Our Lady...That there are all these

different manifestations of God's grace, and you can go from layer to layer and find all these different things.

Ray Fidelez, a 29-year-old administrator at a New York hotel, said that he gained his appreciation for the Latin Mass through studying the philosophy of St. Thomas Aquinas in seminary and college. He dropped out of the traditionalist seminary because it was "too rigid," but he retained a love for the Latin Mass. "When I attended my first Latin Mass, I saw with my eyes what I had already accepted with my intellect. You get the sense that you are doing things that Catholics have always done."[23] John Cuvic said that Catholicism has a "worldview that makes sense. It has an organic tradition lasting 2,000 years. It's satisfying emotionally. It takes all the major events of life and connects them to God. Catholicism guides you the whole way." He added that the reason traditional forms of the faith may be holding more of an appeal to young adults today is because they feel "marooned and stranded in the world of pop culture which homogenizes people. They want to distinguish themselves from bland, interchangeable consumers."

Most of the young adults practiced some forms of Catholic spiritual disciplines, such as praying the rosary, daily prayers, spiritual readings, daily Mass, regular confession and spiritual direction, and fasting. While most of the subjects observed at least one of these disciplines (usually confession), there were sharp differences in the level of involvement in such practices. Tara Aubach has adopted spiritual disciplines that were required before pre-Vatican II, such as abstaining from meat on Fridays and fasting more frequently. She also goes to Mass daily and to confession every two weeks, prays the rosary daily and the angelus and other meditative and contemplative prayers three times a day. She said that through her practice of such disciplines she is becoming devoted to Mary and the saints; approaching Christ and his crucifixion through such devotions is "too awesome" for her and is something that she is working up to very gradually.

Several of the other subjects, such as Aubach's husband, Michael, go to confession irregularly and do not practice the other prayer disciplines on a daily basis. Aubach does not have a spiritual father or confessor, although he thinks he should have one. He and other traditionalists (aside from his wife) tend not to go to daily Mass because such services are usually said in the new rite. While the spiritual disciplines, especially confession, were important for several of the young adults, they were often viewed as forming only one part of the comprehensive faith of the church.

The young adults' appreciation for the richness and comprehensiveness of Catholicism was often accompanied by the emphatic belief that one cannot discard or dissent from church teachings however difficult they may be to follow. Elizabeth Phelan expressed adamant support for the church's prohibition of birth control, saying, "If people sit down and really study [such teachings], they would see the truth of them." Mary Hensel said that the acceptance of contraception in American society has led to acceptance of abortion. Scott Eller said that his acceptance of the church teachings and practice of natural family planning has been the "best thing for my marriage. First of all you're being obedient to God. But also natural family planning promotes communication between couples and gives more meaning to lovemaking."

Michael Aubach said that the "church is one of the last bastions" in "an onslaught of dissent" against such teachings as the prohibition against artificial birth control. Aubach, who does not have children, added that he disagrees with the emphasis in conservative and traditionalist Catholic circles on having big families. "If you don't [have a large family] you are thought to have failed. That seems slanted. I think there was a certain amount of rigidity [in pre-Vatican II Catholicism] that had to be changed. There was a tendency to emphasize the procreative aspect of [sexual relations] more than the unitive aspect. There was a balance missing that's critical." Tara Aubach said that when she first went to speak to a priest about becoming Catholic, she was troubled by the emphasis on rules and regulations, including the prohibition of birth control. "If it's presented as part of a deeper order of things, it's a lot easier to swallow. You can't just tell people to do it. You have to tell them why." At the same time, Aubach stressed the practical benefits of natural family planning. She said the natural method is "extremely effective, but a lot of people don't want to know about it. I know women who are very much into wholistic health and everything natural, but they're also taking the pill. Do they know what they're putting into their body?" She said that her father confessor has advised her that she has no valid reason for not having children, even though she has financial problems. She disagrees. "I feel this is very personal. I'm the only one to know if [her financial situation] is a valid reason. I think I'm in agreement with the Holy See on this."

Battling In The Church

One of the foremost areas of difficulties and concern among all the young adults in their move to a more traditional faith is the liberal influence they have found in the church. When I asked Elizabeth Phelan what she liked least about being Catholic, she answered that she

> feels bad that some Catholics don't understand the truth and they encourage those outside the church to bash it. I don't understand it. If you say you're Catholic and then go against church teachings, why do you want to be part of it? Why bother with belonging if you don't believe it? No one is forcing them to stay

She emphasized the issue of dissent against the church's prohibition of women priests and said that Catholics who disagree with the pope on this matter should go to other denominations that allow such a practice.

Mary Hensel voiced similar criticisms about dissenters and liberals in the church.

> What I hate—and I admit this is a sin—are Catholics who are dissenters; those who accept being Catholic but want it both ways. There has always been a tradition in the church to love one's enemies, but hate the heretics. Maybe that zeal is a holdover from my more evangelical days...What annoys me is that the whole world is going politically correct, and those Catholics pushing for [gender] inclusive language think they're being prophetic. Give me a break! Everyone's doing that.

Hensel added that she does not want war in the church between liberal and conservative Catholics. "It's not war or politics, but an ugly family dispute." She added that the growing anti-Catholicism that she perceives in the New York area may help close ranks between Catholics and discourage internal dissent.

Tara Aubach said that the divisions and dissent in the church present a challenge to her faith. She said that although she is devoted to the Latin Mass, she would not want to impose this on the rest of the church. But she feels that the liberalism of the church has diluted many of the aspects which initially attracted her to the faith.

> Here I am a convert, but I have no opportunity to live [out the faith] in the manner that I imagine living it. I would love to be living in a town where priests wore their cassocks and birettas. Everytime I see a nun in habit, I thank her for wearing it...There are just so many ways in which the church is not supporting what I believe. Look at the acceptance of altar girls [by the Vatican]. It's another friggin' sellout. Nobody says no. It's just so frustrating to be a convert and have to be arguing my faith all the time with other Catholics. It's so strange to put on this new clothing and then be fighting the whole time. There's no chance to luxuriate in it

The sense of struggle and isolation was brought home to Aubach when she recently tried to start a Catholic book club in her neighborhood, where the Catholic classics would be read and discussed. Only one person responded and she wanted to study books by Matthew Fox, a liberal writer who blends New Age with Christian themes. "I ended up really arguing with her about Catholicism and the church; by the time I got off the phone I was actually shaking," Aubach said.

Unlike most of the other young adults, conservative Phillip Holloran criticized parishes and their priests more for their lack of spirituality and holiness than their allowance of dissent. He said that the clergy act like

> it's a popularity contest. The priests, especially the diocesan priests, want to be liked. They're not interested in being obedient to Rome. They need to be more humble, to go back to their vow of poverty, and out of that connect themselves to Christ. The Masses could be a lot more Christ-focused and more intimate.

Scott Eller agreed with Holloran's criticisms, saying that the "non-spiritual aspect of the church bothers me. [Some leaders] don't seem to have a personal relationship with Christ...They can be legalistic or cold and get caught up in too much red tape."

Mary Hensel, like other conservative Catholics, supports Vatican II, but believes it was misinterpreted by liberals who sought drastic reforms in the church. In fact she said that the council's stress on lay involvement in the church has mobilized ordinary lay people "to win back the church. Vatican II really plays into the hands of the conservatives." Echoing the views of other conservative subjects, Hensel said that Pope John Paul II is helping to bring about a restoration of the church. At the same time, the conservative Catholic subjects were equally supportive of ecumenical activities with other conservative churches, particularly the evangelicals. They added, however, that for any genuine church unity to take place, such churches would have to accept the truths of Catholic doctrine.

Cuvic, a strict traditionalist rejected outright many of Vatican II's teachings, such as those on ecumenism and on religious freedom; like many other traditionalists, he called for a revival of Christendom and a Catholic state. Ryan said he views the documents of Vatican II as being intentionally written by some liberal leaders in "vague language designed to be utilized later to bring about liberalization in the church." He added that he is angry that he has to "put up with all this gibberish, the bad architecture, the horrendous music. The U.S. church is in crisis. It's very unpleasant to walk into the average church." He is also disturbed by the church's ecumenical involvement. "The cat has been let out of the bag a long time ago. Let's face it, even if the church joins with Anglicans, there are always going to be other Anglicans who would stay Anglican—you still would not have unity."

Michael Aubach was different from the other traditionalist-oriented Catholics in expressing greater agreement with Vatican II, which he says is in "perfect agreement with Catholic tradition." He added that he is also more "ecumenically-minded" than other traditionalist Catholics. "I'm more inclined to finding common ground with those of like mind. I don't see doctrinal barriers that are significant in light of other things more threatening, such as secularism." He said it is "extremely important to reunite with the Eastern Orthodox. I see the gulf separating us as so small." Tara Aubach said she still "respects a lot of my Buddhist friends," and would disagree with some staunch traditionalists who believe that salvation is only found in the Catholic Church (a view that the Vatican has disavowed). "All these faiths possess part of Christ, but the Catholic Church most completely embodies the truth," she said.

Defending the Faith and the Dissolving Catholic Culture

The task of finding and defending a traditional faith in a pluralistic church ironically becomes part of the process that dissolves the bonds between community and faith. The older pattern (in fact, an obligation) of Catholics belonging to parishes within the boundaries of their neighborhoods is being replaced by a more individualistic and "nontraditional" process of choosing parishes and groups that meet one's needs, or, in the case of the subjects, meet high standards of spirituality and orthodoxy. It could be that these young traditional Catholics, like their more liberal counterparts, no longer view Catholicism in the family-like terms expressed by older Catholics, often expressed in the maxim, "Once Catholic, always Catholic." In other words, the subjects emphasized that correct belief and spiritual vitality is the most important condition for belonging to the church rather than older notions that tied family, ethnic roots and customs closely to a sense of such belonging. Elizabeth Phelan said as much when she expressed her puzzlement about why Catholics who dissent on such doctrines as opposition to women priests choose to remain in the church (although Mary Hensel did say that conflicts on such issues are "ugly family disputes" rather than "wars."). These young adults were not hesitant to criticize bishops and priests who did not uphold Catholic orthodoxy. This critical attitude toward leadership is distinctively modern; criticizing a bishop was itself a sign of unorthodoxy in earlier periods of the church.

The young adults' concern with individual choice and expression could also be seen in their criticisms of Catholic institutions and individuals who are too "rigid" and of priests and other leaders who stress obeying rules (such as on birth control) without explaining why they should be followed. All of this is not to say that the subjects do not experience a sense of community as they gather for their Latin Masses, conservative fellowships and prayer meetings. But these forms of fellowship and worship are communities strongly based on individual choice and belief. The young adults interviewed did not so much want to belong to a tightly knit community as much as they wanted to find a set of beliefs and a source of authority for living which they feel have stood the test of time. This hunger for stability and the timeless authority of the church was pronounced among those devoted to the Latin Mass, but it was present among all the young adults I interviewed. The church's long history in itself functions as what Peter Berger calls a "plausibility structure," something that makes the church an institution worthy of belief and adherence. The view that Catholicism does not change may clash with reality and with official Catholic teachings which emphasize development as well as stability, but it is this ideal of the church's stability amidst periods of tumultuous change that attracted and continues to attract these young adults to Catholicism. Within such a framework of authority, however, the subjects valued the individual freedom and diversity that orthodox Catholicism accommodates to a greater extent than stricter evangelical and fundamentalist churches.

The young adults also spoke of their strong support for the pope (especially, at least among conservatives, the papacy of John Paul II) and the church's claim to have a continuing teaching authority that deserves to be heard and obeyed. It is noteworthy that the church teachings that are the most criticized and under siege by many in the church and society were the most strongly upheld by the subjects. It is difficult not to receive the impression that such teachings as birth control, opposition to women priests, pro-life concerns, and papal authority were often stressed by the young adults because they are the focus of dissent both within and outside of the church today. These doctrines serve as flags which mark out the boundaries of orthodoxy in the "battlefield" of American Catholicism. Michael Cuneo has written that among conservative Catholics, support for such doctrines as papal authority and prohibition of artificial birth control serves to demarcate the line between "true" and "false" Catholics.[24]

At the heart of the conflict between liberal, conservative and traditionalist Catholics is the matter of which party best represents the Catholic tradition today. The young adults hold to the view that the Catholic tradition has been secularized and diluted of its identity. They often criticized liberals as seeking to destroy Catholic tradition and adapt the faith to the ever-changing mores of modern society as they pick and choose items of belief to accept and reject. Liberals and moderates would claim that such a portrayal is a stereotype and would argue that the Catholic tradition is continually developing and changing. Such developments have resulted from interaction with the secular and non-Christian currents of different periods, and such innovators were often initially in conflict with the views of the magisterium and other church officials.

In this view, the attempt to freeze one period in this fluid tradition and hold it up as authoritative or, in the words of Tara Aubach, as the "source" of the faith, such as Tridentine Catholicism and the Latin Mass, is itself a form of selectivity. A return to "tradition" for someone less conservatively inclined can just as easily mean embracing the church of the first five centuries, where there was far less emphasis on papal authority and on a monolithic (Latin) liturgy, or, to go back further, to the more communal and pacifistic church of apostolic times. While this is not the place to enter into a debate about which movement of Catholics best represents Catholic tradition, it should be noted that there is an element of selectivity and choice in the young adults' accounts of retrieving the "true faith" even as they criticize other Catholics for picking and choosing beliefs.

A Struggle With The World And The Flesh

Sitting in a New Jersey diner recounting his conversion story, Steven Kramer, a 24-year-old sales clerk, seemed to be as surprised as anyone else about his recent adoption of Catholicism and the impact it has had on his life. He was brought up in a non-religious Jewish home and considered himself an atheist at least since adolescence. When he was 23 he started dating a young woman who herself was turning to conservative Catholicism. At her encouragement, he started reading the Bible and attending various Protestant and Catholic churches. At one point in reading the Bible, he had the experience that the "words of Jesus were coming from my own conscience, like I had known it all along." He also found himself drawn to the Catholic Church, viewing it as the "most holy" of the churches he had visited. Kramer remembers wanting to receive communion at Catholic churches, but realizing he could not since he was not baptized. In becoming a Catholic, Kramer said he felt he "had come home...It was like being a kid. It just felt like a big relief." But he stressed that he still does not understand why he felt so attracted to Catholicism. Relatives and friends could not understand his conversion and thought he "was crazy." After more than six months Kramer still has not told his father of his conversion since he has a chronic illness and he fears the news might affect his health.

Along with the sense of comfort he finds in his new faith, Kramer also found a good deal of struggle in living out his Catholicism. He admitted that he sometimes has problems with the "authority issue. I've always been distrustful of authority. But it's irrational that I have a problem with it. The church hasn't changed in 2,000 years, and it's all true—that's why I put my trust in it." He often tries to speak to friends and colleagues about his faith, but said he meets misunderstanding and indifference more than opposition. He regrets that his new faith has often made him

> alienate myself from friends and family. I find [the reasons for practicing Catholicism] hard to explain to people...Sometimes I just say, 'it's something I gotta do'...People don't understand being Catholic or being religious. It's like religion is not really important today. It's not preached in the right way. A lot of people think it's just for old people.

He said that the fact that he has approached his faith on a more individualistic basis and does not have a strong support system of a parish and role models (although he does attend a parish prayer meeting), makes practicing his faith more difficult.[25]

Like Kramer, most of the young adults spoke of the difficulties in practicing their faith in the wider society. Some subjects, such as Scott Eller and Elizabeth Phelan, are outspoken about their faith among co-workers, although they feel discrimination for being vocal about this aspect of their lives. Others, such as James Ryan, keep their faith private in work and social situations.

> I don't feel comfortable blessing myself in public, or saying the Rosary. I'm very private in my faith life...It takes too much energy bringing up the subject and always having to explain it...It's going against the stream, and you often don't want to hurt peoples' feelings [by arguing with them about beliefs].

Tara Aubach said that while she tries to speak to others about her Catholic faith, she still feels uncomfortable about it. At this point in the interview, she pulled a date book out of her back pack with a picture of the Virgin Mary on the front cover and said that she often feels hesitant to show it to non-Catholic friends. Aubach added that a reason for her reticence about the faith may be because "I grew up in a family where being a Catholic was the worst thing you could be."

While her parents are not as opposed to her being Catholic as they were at first, they still find it difficult to accept.

Most of the conservative Catholic subjects changed their circle of friends to largely consist of fellow Catholics since adopting the faith. They also made important changes in their lifestyles. Kramer has made a strong break from his previous life when he was involved in drinking and drugs and was sexually active. He is no longer close to many of his non-believing friends and has mostly Catholic friends. He is living a celibate life, but finds it difficult. Kramer was brought up on television and watched a lot of it, but today he has cut his viewing habits drastically, mainly because of TV's "objectionable" content. Kramer feels that his faith also conflicts with his former enjoyment of hard rock music; in fact, he does not listen to much music anymore. Catholic books, particularly those on the saints, occupy most of his reading. Phelan changed from listening to secular rock to contemporary Christian rock music. Phillip Halloran was more accepting of secular music, but, like the other conservative young adults, sharply curtailed his viewing of television and movies and videos with sexual themes and imagery.

The traditionalist-oriented young adults devoted to the Latin Mass were more accepting than the conservatives of various forms of modern popular culture, such as rock music and R-rated films were more likely to have non-Catholic friendships. Tara Aubach said that she while she is more careful today about what she watches and listens to, she does not want to be a "puritan" and draw up a list of rules and regulations to follow. She still listens to jazz, classical and rock and roll music. She is not opposed to R-rated films on principle, but added that she is "more sensitive to the impact things have on you. I try to keep myself apart from the surrounding culture." Most of her friends are non-Catholics, although she noted that her more recent friends tend to believe in God. The fact that she also works in a bookstore in Manhattan that caters to lesbians presents some dilemmas to her faith, though not to the degree that one might expect. She said she has become close friends with her lesbian coworkers, although sometimes such relations are strained because "they can't handle what I'm believing."

Her work in modern dance also causes conflicts because it is "difficult to maintain a Christian outlook" in such an art form that is closely tied to modern culture. "I feel that I should do more to honor

God in dance, that there should be more purpose to it. I'm thinking about setting the lives of saints to dance," she said. Although many fellow parishioners would frown on her involvement in such activities, Aubach said that she is trying to serve as a "beacon" to non-believers. John Cuvic reports on new developments in technology for a business magazine and sees little conflict between such work and his traditionalist Catholicism. He does, however, tend to stay away from strictly business-related issues because of the magazine's emphasis on the "Protestant work ethic," which he sees as being in conflict with his idea of Catholic culture. Scott Eller sees "a lot of greed" in his work as a stock broker. "It seems like the very nature of the job is sinful. I'm selling greed...There's not as much connection between my faith and job as I would like." Eller sees his work in the investment firm as a "means to an end"—providing him with enough income to live "comfortably" so he can eventually move to full-time lay work with the poor and homeless.

A significant area of lifestyle change among the Catholic young adults centered on sexuality and romantic relationships. Since her move to conservative Catholicism, Phelan has changed her relations with men from being fairly sexually active to remaining celibate until she marries. Too often young people "fall into sexual relations before they even really know each other," she said. Phelan added she is not as conscious of physical attractiveness in men as she once was and is now more attracted to men who have a "strong faith." Mary Hensel finds dating more difficult since becoming a conservative Catholic because her "total involvement" in Catholicism has become a barrier for non-Catholics. As with most of the other single subjects, she prefers to marry a Catholic. Her strong opposition to premarital sex is not just a private concern. When she was considering rooming with a nominal Catholic friend, Hensel insisted that no men should be allowed to sleep over, since it would be allowing mortal sin to take place under her roof. The friend disagreed with such a condition and called the deal off. Phillip Holloran said that while he was never strongly involved in sexual activity when he was younger, today he is more likely to value a "spiritual" quality in women and not be "distracted" by physical appearances. He now believes that it is a "sin to kiss someone to [the point of] sexual arousal."

Hensel said that her strictness on sexuality may be due to the influence evangelicals had on her when she was growing up. She may be right. As with their greater acceptance of modern culture, traditionalist-oriented singles such as Ray Fidelez and Cuvic tended to be less strict in their sexual behavior than their conservative counterparts. Both subjects said they have been sexually active since entering their 20s. Fidelez said that during the 1980s, he was a "club kid," or a regular at Manhattan night clubs. He compared his indulgence in sexual activity to eating cake: "I love cake, but if you have too much you get fat." Today, he enjoys the company mainly of traditional Catholics and "hedonistic people" who have no beliefs and values at all. "Those are the only two groups of people who are consistent [in their beliefs]," Fidelez said. While Cuvic said that his sexual activity is a sin and he confesses it as such in confession, he does not emphasize sexual conduct as being more serious than other sins, such as gluttony and uncharitable behavior. He said traditionalists tend to be more "freewheeling" and that conservatives tend to be "puritan" and put a greater stress on sexual sins over other sins.

Defensive Politics

Almost all of the subjects held to strongly conservative political and social positions. Several said they enjoyed listening to the conservative talk show host Rush Limbaugh. Often their political views were shaded by pessimism, as subjects voiced distrust of politicians and suspicion about state involvement in their lives. Phelan said she "stays away from politics. On the high level everything seems corrupt." She is a Republican but usually votes for Right to Life party candidates. Steven Kramer said that he "tries to keep out of politics. Last election, I just voted Right to Life [candidates]. I'm just trying to live a simple life. I don't have much faith that politics will do anything." Yet most of the young adults reported that they are more interested in political concerns since moving to orthodox Catholicism, usually focusing on such issues as abortion and other family issues. Other issues addressed in Catholic social teachings, such as involvement in local political activism, war and peace issues, or the labor movement, were rarely mentioned by them.

Hensel said that on a national scale, especially during the Clinton administration, Catholics are "drawing back more and more from supporting the U.S. government. I don't think we're trusting the government as much as we use to...We're more loyal to the church than to government." This negative view of the government was expressed in the kinds of political involvement concern engaged in by these young adults. For instance, they strongly protested the state giving "special privileges" to homosexuals through anti-discrimination laws, the expansion of the welfare state, and the public schools being the sole provider of education. James Ryan reflected much of the subjects' political mindset. He is against gay rights, but would not want to see homosexuals persecuted or discriminated against. He said that "parents rights" are often trampled upon in giving rights to such unconventional minorities. In his view, parents have the right to bring up their children without high taxes and social influences that would undermine the family, such as the "homosexual agenda."

Ryan and the two other married young adults strongly opposed sending their prospective children to public schools. Ryan said that he would not likely send his children to parochial school because he disapproves of their "liberal" sex education programs. He and his wife, who is a teacher, plan to school their children at home through a new Catholic home-schooling program. Tara Aubach said she would only send her children to "an orthodox parochial school I can trust" or teach them at home. While Scott Eller said he opposes much in the public schools, he is uncertain whether to send his son to a parochial school, a "quality" public school or instruct him at home.

Although Tara Aubach has homosexual friends she said that there should not be laws protecting homosexuals rights, "just as there shouldn't be laws protecting adulterers' rights." But she added that she would also not want laws outlawing homosexual activity. "I'm leery of laws. I'm turned off by something that would be the reverse of gay rights laws...I'm really ambiguous about how Catholics should create change." Her husband Michael said he would not want to discriminate against homosexuals by law but added that there should be a way of "putting social pressure on communities to not sanction bad behavior. The same thing was done with teenage pregnancy in the 1950s. In some ways it's unjust, but the greater good is being served. The social order is being kept intact."

Many of the subjects doubted the effectiveness of outlawing abortion, even though they have been involved in such efforts and support the church's position against legal abortion. Even such a traditionalist as Cuvic who believes in restoring a Catholic state, said that on abortion it is more important to change people's attitudes than the laws in order to alleviate the problem. Michael Aubach said that while he "ideally supports a Constitutional amendment prohibiting abortion, I think the only way to stop it will be through changing people's minds. I don't think there is a legal solution to it." While she has been strongly involved in anti-abortion marches and protests and favors making abortion illegal, Phelan made much the same point, saying, "making laws isn't going to change things."

All of the young adults saw capitalism as the best economic system available; problems such as greed and poverty were attributed more to growing immorality in society than to deficiencies in the free market system itself. They strongly disapproved of affirmative action programs that seek to redress social inequalities by enforcing "quotas" of minorities in employment and education. There was little acceptance of Catholic leaders' criticisms of capitalism. James Ryan said he "abhorred" the U.S. Catholic bishops' letters on the economy and nuclear arms. Rather than becoming involved in social issues, the bishops should "put their own house in order." He said he considers the church's teachings on "personal behavior" more binding than teachings on economics and issues such as the labor movement. Even the minority of subjects who agreed with much of what the U.S. bishops had to say in their statements on the economy and war and peace, such as Michael Aubach and Mary Hensel, said they had not studied the documents nor were they an important part of their Catholic life or identity. Only Phelan and Phillip Holloran came out against the death penalty, saying that their pro-life position would not allow them to accept such a measure. Other subjects were either undecided or saw the death penalty as serving as a deterrent against murder. None of the young adults, including the opponents of capital punishment, cited the U.S. Catholic bishops' opposition to the death penalty in speaking on this issue. Holloran was also more accepting of government welfare programs and peace concerns than the other subjects. His involvement in the Medjugorje Marian movement, where the Marian messages often call for peace, may have been a factor in his concern for world peace.

While there was an acceptance of democracy and religious freedom among most young adults, there was (often at the same time) some admiration for a Catholic state, at least as an ideal. Hensel said, "I don't think the Middle Ages were that bad. With [reestablishing]

Christendom, you do have a whole set of problems you would have to deal with, but most of it seems valid." Michael Aubach said that he "would love to live in a Catholic state, and maybe 30 years ago it was possible. But today you have to be starry-eyed to believe that could happen." The young adults often expressed their political views in defensive or even war-like terms, sometimes referring to impending martyrdom for the faith. Hensel said she supports joining evangelicals in a "culture war," over such issues as abortion and gay rights, and says that "a lot of my friends even talk about dying as martyrs...I think we are coming into a time of martyrdom. But the church has always thrived when the call to arms has been sounded. It's a great time to be Catholic."

Hensel added that the church has to be as intense and militant as the secular culture. "It's as Pope John Paul says: 'Youth is not made for self-indulgence. Youth is made for heroism.' When young people hear that they go to it like moths to a flame. Those churches that emphasize faith as a journey or a matter of seeking are not going to attract anyone." The other young adults also said that being a Catholic is increasingly a struggle and that there is a rising tide of anti-Catholicism in American society. Phelan said such anti-Catholicism developed "mostly because of the media." She said the media is anti-Catholic because the "church represents authority, because it tells people what to do." She added that in today's world, the young people especially are "becoming too independent. The church is showing that community is important rather than individualism."

Feminism and the roles of the sexes was a central concern among all the young adults. The men agreed that gender roles have become too blurred in modern society and that women and men have different roles, especially in the home. Traditionalist Ray Fidelez said that men and women have "certain roles," such as that women were meant to nurture and raise children, while men were intended to provide for their families. Scott Eller said that in the home, "the husband is the king, but he's a just king. He is commanded by God to be fair, to look out for others' interests, not his own." Eller favored equality for women in society, but said that "motherhood is the most honored profession," and that women with children should stay home to raise them. The women, however, were just as outspoken in their opposition to feminism. Phelan said the "feminist movement did more to damage women than men ever did. Feminists are just awful. They want us to become men and seem unhappy about being women. The women priest thing [women being ordained as priests] is just awful." Phelan said that she supports such measures as equal pay for women and men. Men and women are equal in marriage, but "they are also different...men are called to take a greater leadership role in the family," she added.

Echoing such comments, Hensel said,

> I was judged by feminism and found wanting. All through school, I was pushed toward masculine attributes, such as being good at athletics, pushed to be aggressive. But who can compete with guys? It gave me lower self-esteem. I found myself liking more feminine aspects of things, but it was not at all encouraged. Finding the Catholic view of womanhood gave me freedom. I didn't have to do those things...There's nothing wrong with being protected by a man.

She said that while being submissive to a husband might be difficult, "the husband has to act like Christ, which is much harder." Tara Aubach said that the man's role is to "represent the family in the world, while the women takes care of the family in the home." She added that "when you really look at who's holding the reigns in the family, it's usually the women." She also said that the women should feel free to work "if it's not affecting the children."

Creating A Catholic Counterculture

The conservative and traditional Catholic young adults are fighting a battle on two fronts; they are in conflict with the liberalism and pluralism they find within the institutional church, while also struggling with the secularism they find in society. In their accounts of seeking and finding a traditional faith, the subjects often expressed themselves in terms of struggle, and even combat with the wider society, whether over gay rights or suspected anti-Catholicism. Elizabeth Phelan astutely picked up on the undercurrent of conflict between so much of American society and the Catholic Church when she said that anti-Catholicism is present because "the church represents authority, because it tells people what to do." Even though most of the subjects are involved in one way or another in the pro-life movement, many of them expressed doubt about whether new laws can substantially change the abortion situation. These subjects appear to have accepted the view that changing society through laws is difficult at best, especially in a society that is increasingly pluralistic. This implicit acceptance of cultural pluralism is evident in the subjects' ability to adapt to modern society (especially within the context of New York City and environs) while also—often at the same time—being in conflict with it. Tara Aubach is able to juggle the clashing cultures of her traditionalist-oriented parish life and modern dance and her work in a lesbian bookstore; John Cuvic writes enthusiastically about technology while disdaining the idea of the Protestant work ethic. There was also a general acceptance of religious pluralism and little desire to attack other faiths.

The young adults' attitudes to feminism and gender roles provide an example of how they balanced the conservative aspects of their faith with a more modern approach that accommodated contemporary challenges and realities. Both male and female subjects stressed the differences between the sexes and that men should provide a leadership role in the home while women should nurture the children. At the same time, most of the male and female subjects supported women having careers and agreed—especially the females—that husbands and wives are equal in marriage. The subjects were either unaware or unconcerned that the widely accepted teaching that women should be in submission to their husbands has been revised by Pope John Paul II himself; in other words, they are selecting a "traditional" view that is in the process of being replaced by the same tradition that they champion.[26] Despite their fidelity to Rome, these young adults accepted and stressed the older view of marriage relations for a reason: such a view provides a stronger bulwark against what they see as increasing challenges to traditional gender roles.

The idea of a Catholic state or even Catholic politics and values imposed by law (or from above) was not seriously entertained by most of the subjects. There was much more attention paid to what has been called defensive politics—battling for one's own space to practice the faith and protecting oneself against intrusions from the secularistic, "anti-Christian" world, whether it be the state or the media. The subjects' dislike and curtailment of television viewing appeared to be a popular protest against such an intrusion. Throughout the interviews, there was little mention of the more public aspects of Catholic teachings and how they might influence their neighborhoods or society in more positive ways. This may be because such close-at-hand concerns as gender roles hold greater resonance for people in this age group than more distant social issues, such as war and peace, worker's rights, or opposition to the death penalty. But, more importantly, feminism, abortion, gay rights and other contested issues are part of today's "culture wars," a conflict over which values will inform society—a battle in which the Catholic Church has become a major protagonist. It would be incorrect to say the subjects are socially unconcerned. Rather, the area of social concern has shifted from international issues (i.e., human rights) to local ones that have become increasingly targeted by an ascendant conservative Catholic leadership.

Following the lead of Pope John Paul II, the young adults spoke of Catholicism as serving as a counterculture that is in basic conflict with much of the rest of American society. Conservative Catholic leaders and writers increasingly speak of Catholicism as forsaking an older model of "assimilation"—trying to make Catholic concerns and identity blend with American culture—for a countercultural posture that would put the accent of Catholic distinctiveness in an increasingly pluralistic American society.[27] The Catholic young adults exemplify this change of attitude and strategy in their attitudes and lifestyles, although, as noted above, their individualistic patterns of religious practice and affiliation may make the formation of a vital counterculture difficult to achieve. As the culture wars described above are influenced by and reflected in shifts in political life, it may well be that many of the countercultural concerns of these young adults will be addressed by the emerging conservative Republican leadership which was elected in 1994. Such a change in political leadership, however, will not necessarily affect changes in gender relations, gay rights, abortion and other moral issues. But the election may have signaled that some of the concerns of the subjects (especially their criticism of welfare and support for school vouchers) are no longer so countercultural but rather are receiving mainstream support.

The Lost Generation

Throughout the interviews there were frequent references as to how the older generations, particularly the baby boomers, have affected the young adults' generation. Such references may have been made because the subjects realized they were taking part in a study of young adults. Whatever the reason, they did not have a high view of the baby boomers preceding them. Hensel said,

> I don't like [baby boomers], even though my parents are in the generation. They raised flagships in society that were very damaging. Only baby boomers would try to fight AIDS with condoms. It's the whole idea that you can't live without sex. They affected the trend toward the whole pick-and-choose type of Catholicism.

During parochial high school, Hensel found herself in conflict with the nuns, although, in turning the tables on Catholic folklore, it was not because of their strictness. "I had a real problems with the nuns. They always used to yell at me telling me I was too strict, to let my hair down, loosen up." Today, Phelan often sees "young orthodox Catholics witnessing to people in their 40s and 50s who got psyched out on Vatican II." Ryan added that "So many [of the baby boomer and older generations] were so attracted to Catholicism that they became celibate...What puzzles me is that these same people did so much to dismantle the great church that they made a commitment to." Cuvic put the matter more dramatically, saying, that "generation X (or twentysomethings) missed the utopianism of the 60s and the utopianism of Vatican II. We didn't get drunk. We just got the hangover, we are the hangover. The legacy of the 60s is empty churches, schools and seminaries."

The culture wars and church conflict described by the young adults take place within as well as between generations. But they blamed much of what they think is wrong today on the decade of the 60s, a period when the oldest of the subjects were still small children. The young adults I interviewed emphasized the view that they were robbed of Catholic traditions by the baby boomers in their quest for innovation and change. This view is common among young Catholic conservatives and traditionalists, finding clearest expression in the writings of traditionalist Charles Coulombe. But even more liberal young Catholics frequently view themselves, in the words of writer Jennifer Bradley, as the "lost generation of Catholics" and lament the lack of strong religious formation they received growing up in the post-Vatican II church. In a noteworthy article in the *New Republic*, Bradley writes that in religious education classes during her high school years, "church history, elementary theology, even basic Bible study was pre-empted by nuclear war or sex. The Church was against both." Bradley adds that she cannot even intelligently dissent from church teachings because she is untutored in the basics of Catholicism.

> Those of who grew up in safe suburbs with safe public schools, or in Sunbelt cities where there was no Ursuline school for girls and no Jesuit school for boys, have a child's spirituality. True, Jesus said that to come to Him we should be like children, but no doubt he meant childish innocence, not childish ignorance.[28]

The generation gap takes on a greater meaning in American Catholicism than in other faiths. A youth revolution was taking place in the wider society at the same time that a religious revolution was being fomented in the church. The revolution known as Vatican II was not started or implemented by baby boomers, but it found special resonance among a crowded generation which embraced the idea of change. The 60s generation's restlessness and sense of open horizons in lifestyles and social experimentation gave way to a mood marked by limits, especially as the results of such experiments did not always live up to their promise. In the accounts of conversion and return to orthodox Catholicism among these young adults, one hears loud refrains of disenchantment with radical change as well as a call to rebel against the rebellions of the 1960s.

Wade Clark Roof notes that those born between 1946 and 1954 experienced the social movements of the 1960s head-on. They were "challengers" ready to take on the establishment, and they viewed "chaotic change as revolution or as revelation." The younger cohort born between 1955 and 1962 came of age in a quieter time marked by recession, and Watergate. They are called "calculators," intent upon "setting priorities to go after in a world where you cannot have it all."[29] The subjects' concentration on local issues and skepticism about large-scale political change can be interpreted as a kind of calculation, as is Scott Eller's plans to work with the homeless while making enough money as a stock broker to insure a "comfortable" life. But as much as the young adults want to disassociate themselves from the older baby boomers, they share with their older siblings an individualistic approach to faith, one that emphasizes aggressively seeking the truth and creating a place for oneself in a pluralistic church.

CHAPTER 2:
The Reformed Tradition

A recent study shows that the majority of those in the baby boom generation who were raised in the Presbyterian Church (USA) have not returned to the fold. To add to church leaders' discomfort, those who have come back to the church, which was once the main bearer of the Calvinist tradition, are often unaware and uninterested in the teachings of John Calvin.[1] Such findings should not be particularly surprising since most mainline Reformed denominations no longer require adherence to the classical Calvinist creeds and confessions. Although there are many self-confessing Calvinists within such bodies, the declining membership rolls of mainline denominations associated with Calvinism or the Reformed tradition is enough to make one think that Calvinism is destined for marginality if not extinction among the younger generations.

A closer examination of the ebb and flow of denominational growth, however, reveals that the rumors of Calvinism's death are greatly exaggerated; the tradition has not died, but it has branched out and taken on new forms. Such denominations as the Presbyterian Church in America, the Orthodox Presbyterian Church, the Christian Reformed Church, and the Reformed Episcopal Church are all conservative bodies that hold to the historic Calvinist creeds, such as the Westminster Confession of Faith. Most of these denominations have experienced steady growth (if not the explosive increases found in more experienced-based evangelical groups such as the charismatics); for instance the Presbyterian Church in America has grown from approximately 211,000 members in 1988 to about 250,000 in 1993.[2] There are also numerous independent congregations espousing orthodox Calvinism and a growing Calvinist movement within the Southern Baptist Convention and among other Baptist churches (which are often called Reformed Baptist). Some of the largest Presbyterian congregations in the country, such as the Coral Ridge Presbyterian Church in Fort Lauderdale, Florida, belong to these conservative bodies.

While there are no reliable figures on the number of young adults involved in conservative Calvinism, it appears that the number is high. Nearly 65 percent of the readership of the Reformed-oriented magazine *World* (with a circulation of about 60,000) are baby boomers or busters. Seminaries and colleges which are connected to this conservative Reformed movement, such as the Reformed Theological Seminary, Westminster Seminary (both seminaries have branches in different parts of the U.S.) and Geneva College in Pennsylvania, have shown similar signs of vitality and growth. The steady growth rates of most conservative Reformed bodies suggest that young people are being drawn to these groups. One Reformed editor said it is "very typical" for conservative Reformed congregations to draw young families to its pews, especially because Calvinist theology emphasizes the role of the family in the covenant God made with his church. The most important transmitter of the faith in the conservative Reformed faith is not so much the pastor as the father of each family.[3] Many conservative Calvinist-oriented thinkers and activists, such as George Grant, Marvin Olasky and Randall Terry, are baby boomers or younger. Reformed thought continues to find a hearing on evangelical campuses, and young Calvinists are influential participants in pro-life activism.

Most of the conservative Reformed denominations are the result of schisms from larger mainline bodies during periods when the orthodoxy of a parent denomination was called into question, such as during the fundamentalist-modernist conflict in the early 20th century. The birth of the Orthodox Presbyterian Church in 1936 stemmed from the bitter battle between conservatives and liberals in the Presbyterian Church in the U.S.A. over such issues as the inerrancy of the Bible and the authority of the historic Reformed confessions. Founded by eminent theologian J. Gresham Machen of Princeton Theological Seminary, the Orthodox Presbyterian Church saw itself as safeguarding the Calvinist truths that its parent body was diluting in the process of modernizing its theology.

The Reformed tradition in America has been both wide and deep. It has embraced the Congregational churches started by the Puritans in New England, Reformed immigrants and refugees from continental Europe, the Presbyterianism of British settlers, and a segment of Episcopalians and Baptists. Uniting these disparate groups have been their confessions of faith and catechisms which have sought to elucidate and pass on what have been called the "doctrines of grace." This confessional thrust has historically set Reformed churches apart from other evangelical Protestants, such as the Methodists, Baptists and Pentecostals, who have put more emphasis on Christian living and experience than on creeds and doctrine. The smaller Reformed bodies mentioned above have sought to return to the letter as well as the spirit of these confessions, providing them with a strongly conservative theology.

Such doctrines would include biblical inerrancy, holding that the Bible is reliable in all matters of doctrine and history. Conservative Calvinists of all kinds view biblical authority as the foundation on which all their creeds and theologizing stands. Other keystones of the conservative Reformed tradition include: the total sinfulness of humans; that God's choosing of the elect for salvation is unconditional, having nothing to do with our own deeds; that God's will is sovereign and that a person cannot resist his grace when chosen for salvation; in other words, there is no freewill. More liberal Reformed groups have interpreted these doctrines in a less literal way, but it is important to stress that all Reformed theology is very much centered on God and his power and sovereignty over his creation.

Related to this theology is the view that throughout history God deals with humans through "covenants" by which he enters into special relations with particular groups or nations, such as in his dealings with Israel in the Old Testament. More than most Protestant traditions, the Reformed faith has a strong base in the Old Testament, holding that God's covenant with Israel is a model for the church today and that Old Testament laws, particularly the Ten Commandments, are applicable to Christians and to society at large. The strict practice of refraining from work and play on Sunday, or the Sabbath, among conservative Calvinist believers is another indication of the impact of biblical law in their lives. A more recent teaching among conservative Calvinists is that of the "antithesis." This teaching, formulated by American theologian Cornelius Van Til, holds that there is a radical difference between Christians and non-Christians and that there is no way that unregenerate people can grasp Christianity on their own. Therefore Christians should not seek a middle ground or appeal to reason with unbelievers, but rather present them with scriptural truth and let the Holy Spirit work. Such a teaching has reinforced the historic emphasis of expository preaching of the Bible in Reformed worship.

The Reformed confidence that God is sovereign over the universe and that his laws should be applied to society has made Calvinists culturally and politically active throughout history. From John Calvin's theocracy in Geneva to today's conservative Calvinists in the forefront of the pro-life movement, Reformed believers have sought to transform cultures. The Calvinists have had an equally strong impact on contemporary American Christianity. Among evangelicals, Reformed believers are known as the intellectuals (one evangelical magazine referred to Dutch Calvinists as "our Orthodox Jews"), often preferring to elucidate fine points of doctrine while their more pragmatic and experience-oriented counterparts are leading evangelistic crusades. As evangelicals increasingly move to more experiential forms of the faith, such as in entertainment and "seeker"-oriented megachurches and emphasizing teaching methods over preaching, the Reformed tradition appears to be increasingly out of step with the rest of evangelicalism.

In recent decades, the Calvinists have been very influential in drawing non-Reformed evangelicals into greater political and cultural involvement. Church historian George Marsden points out that after World War II, Dutch Calvinists introduced American evangelicals to the thought of Abraham Kuyper, a turn-of-the-century Dutch theologian and politician who emphasized the role of Calvinism in transforming culture and bringing society more into line with God's law. The impact of Kuyper's ideas among evangelicals led a new generation to speak of developing a "Christian worldview" when trying to relate their faith to a wide range of knowledge and activities. Until the 1970s, the Reformed influence among evangelicals was often considered to be liberal, as it convinced pietistic, apolitical believers to become more concerned and involved in "worldly" matters. Such a thinker as Francis Schaeffer sought to translate Calvinistic concepts into the popular cultural idiom of searching Christians and non-Christians in the late 1960s and early 70s, as he sought to develop a

Christian view of art, literature, and politics. The Dutch Calvinist Reformed Journal was seen as the leading evangelical intellectual publication for its in-depth cultural and political coverage.

Marsden notes, however, that by the mid-70s

> such moderately conservative emphases were converging with the resurgence of conservative politics among American fundamentalists and fundamentalistic evangelicals. Versions of Kuyperian Calvinism such as those suggested by [Schaeffer] in the influential political ministry of his later years helped articulate the new fundamentalist conservative emphases of the Moral Majority.[4]

The call to restore a "Christian America" by the New Christian Right dovetailed with the Calvinist emphasis on Christianizing culture, especially in its more conservative versions. Schaeffer had become strongly involved in the pro-life movement by that time, even moving to the point of advocating civil disobedience against government when it violates biblical morality. At the same time, a movement of conservative Calvinists calling for a radical restructuring of American society according to the Bible—particularly the Old Testament—was gaining a following. Under such thinkers as Rousas Rushdoony and Gary North, the movement known as "theonomy" or Christian reconstructionism had a strong impact on the smaller conservative Calvinist bodies, such as the Orthodox Presbyterian Church and the Presbyterian Church in America.

All of these currents taken together created a revival of conservative Calvinist thinking and action in the 1980s. The new Calvinism is anti-statist and pro-free market, strongly in favor of Christian and home schooling, and aggressive in attacking secularism and liberalism in all quarters, including within the wider evangelical movement. This new Calvinist activism also found a hearing among non-Calvinists, such as Pentecostal pro-life activist Randall Terry of Operation Rescue, and has come to be known as the Christian worldview movement. The Christian worldview critique of church and society is carried by a diversity of organizations, such as the evangelical newsweekly *World* and Crossway Books. By distancing itself from extreme forms of Christian reconstructionist thought, the movement is likely to gain continuing influence in the evangelical world.[5]

The 10 young adults the reader will be meeting in the pages ahead represent the "mainstream" of the conservative Reformed movement, while also showing its diversity on such doctrinal issues as baptism and reconstructionism. The subjects were chosen from three congregations representing the Orthodox Presbyterian, independent Reformed and Reformed Baptist traditions.

Giving God The Glory

Driving his car around the side streets of Staten Island as he went about his work as an insurance appraiser, Anthony Genelli often reached for the tattered Bible he kept in the back seat, looking up passages to buttress his comments about what he liked best about the Reformed faith. "Everything is equally emphasized in the Reformed tradition, the Old Testament, the New Testament; it's comprehensive," said Genelli during the interview. "What I like best about the Reformed faith is the sovereignty of God. It's comforting to know that God is in control. If I had control of my life it would go to pot." Aside from the location of his interview, Genelli was not unusual among the Reformed young adults. Hardly any of my interviews with young adult Calvinists ended before they had opened a well-worn Bible or copy of the Westminster Catechism to defend or elucidate a particular view they had expressed. They were doing more than proof-texting; the young Calvinists seemed to carry on a constant internal conversation with the biblical text.

Genelli, a 31-year-old member of the Orthodox Presbyterian Church, grew up as a Catholic and attended parochial schools. He stopped practicing his faith after his confirmation, believing that while Catholicism taught him the "essentials" it did not reach him on a spiritual level. In high school he became involved in the "world of rock music, girls and drugs." He was a musician for several years, until his dreams of success were crushed. He was paid to go to London and cut a record but at the last minute the deal was called off. "I was unfulfilled in my hope for a career. After that I didn't care about things." He said during this time, he was reading a lot about different religions. Finding inconsistencies in non-Christian religions, Genelli became a born again Christian when he was 26 through the encouragement of his brother. While he was attending a Bible study at a charismatic church, his brother started going to an Orthodox

Presbyterian congregation. When Genelli visited the church, he felt "uncomfortable. It didn't feel right. It was too stiff and formal." At the advice of the pastor he started attending an independent Reformed congregation that had more young people. "They were down-to-earth. There was a lot more community and fellowship there." He especially liked the church's pastor, who was a Jewish convert. "He was a perfectionist...It was appealing to see a guy who was not a flim-flam, not wishy-washy." A women he was dating went with him to the services, but he said she was "too wild...We used to go back to my apartment and have sex after church." They parted ways after Genelli became increasingly involved in the church and decided he did not "want anything to do with the world."[6]

Like Genelli, most of the young adults grew up as nominal members of mainline Protestant and Catholic churches (several attended Catholic parochial schools). In their teen years and early twenties, they were introduced to evangelical Christianity, usually through a friend or relative. After attending an evangelical church, such as Baptist or charismatic, for a period they came into contact with a Reformed church or Reformed teachings. Often this experience of coming to the Reformed faith was like a second conversion for the subjects. "It [moving from an evangelical congregation to the Orthodox Presbyterian Church] was as different as moving from the Catholic Church to an evangelical church," said Bill Wenzel, a 32-year-old chef. Wenzel, a former Baptist, said that it was something of a shock when he first attended the Orthodox Presbyterian Church.

> When I first heard Reformed preaching it felt offensive. I had to wrestle with what I heard. Things that may have been offensive [to preach about] in my Baptist church, like about hell and that all of us are deserving of God's wrath, were preached openly....Christ was preached in all his fullness.[7]

When Christine Ishuwa, a 31-year-old dancer and dance teacher, first heard a Reformed sermon in a Presbyterian church in California as a college student, she said it was a "mind-blowing experience...The preaching was so biblical. The words the pastor was speaking were true. It was incredible." Ishuwa had grown up in the liberal United Church of Christ and had become an evangelical in college.[8] Most of the subjects said they felt they were coming face-to-face with biblical teachings for the first time, especially with the Old Testament, which was neglected in their previous churches. Tom Ferre, a 32-year-old art director, said what drew him to the Orthodox Presbyterian Church was that "doctrine was important to them, and that they walked the walk as well as talked the talk." His wife, Julie, added that "whenever I had questions the pastor always answered them from scripture and from the fathers of the faith in the Westminster Confession."[9] As Julie Ferre's remark suggests, the subjects distinguished themselves from many evangelicals who put an emphasis on "the Bible alone," disregarding the role of creeds and confessions in understanding biblical truths. Their emphasis on biblical teaching was accompanied by a strong appreciation of the role of tradition and history in rightly interpreting and handing down the faith. Charles Dornan, a 30-year-old executive for a Christian radio station who attends a Reformed Baptist congregation, said that, unlike many evangelical churches, the Reformed tradition "benefits from the great Protestants of history. Most evangelicals scoff at tradition, at the Puritans and the Reformers." He added that Reformed Baptist churches, unlike many other Baptists, have their own confessions—known as the London Confession of Faith from the 17th century—which provides a link to other Calvinist bodies.[10]

After hearing subjects expound on the importance of law and doctrine, I was surprised by some of their answers when I asked them what they liked most about being Reformed. "I feel freer," Ishuwa replied. "The Reformed faith teaches that everything God made is good. Before [in being a member of other evangelical churches] you couldn't smoke or drink. With being Reformed you could take a glass or wine or smoke if you want to." Julie Ferre said she appreciates the Reformed tradition's emphasis "that it's all of grace. There was too much emphasis on doing good works [in evangelical churches] rather than on God who gives you the desire to do good works."

Cynthia Balen, a 28-year-old college instructor who is a member of the Reformed Baptist congregation, also cited the emphasis on God's power and sovereignty as the most appealing aspect of the Reformed tradition. Balen came to the congregation with her husband after a period of disenchantment with the non-Calvinistic Baptist faith she had adopted when she was a teenager. The dissatisfaction she felt was intensified when she attended a Billy Graham crusade in which her church was involved. "It was very numbers-oriented, very professional. Instead of letting the spirit of God deal with people's hearts, the meetings were like a performance" in order to draw in converts. After such encounters, Balen became increasingly attracted to the Reformed faith, which puts less attention on getting results, such as converting large numbers of people, and "gives God all the glory, she added. Like the other subjects, Balen said she no longer feels the pressure to use the right techniques and strategies to convert people, but rather leaves the results up to God.[11]

Predestination, the teaching that God elects people for salvation apart from freewill, was often the most difficult doctrine to accept for most young adults, but it became one of the most appreciated teaching once they become more involved in the Reformed tradition. Sally Michael, a 32-year-old administrator at the independent Reformed church, became a born-again Christian at a college in Oregon and became involved in an evangelical Baptist church. In moving back to her home in New York, she was drawn to a Reformed church for the biblical truth she said she found there. The teachings on predestination that Michael heard in the church at first sounded "radical" to her, but on a second examination she found that they complimented her own views she held since childhood. "As a kid, I always thought about things like that. Can I do anything of my own free will, or was I meant to do certain things, like stepping on the crack of a sidewalk?...So what [I heard from the preaching in the Reformed church] answered these questions."[12]

Anthony Genelli said of predestination that "It's my greatest comfort now, but it was my greatest problem—that God elects some to be saved and not others. But it's true. We're all pawns in God's game. There's no freewill." After some struggle on the doctrine, Ishuwa came to the view that "It's extremely God-glorifying, that God didn't just create the world and then leave it, but that he is always acting, that everything is predetermined in it....It's very comforting—that God created me for a purpose and that I have an end." Tom Ferre also wrestled with the doctrine and after studying the Bible he concluded that "it takes the emphasis off man and puts it on God. Throughout the Bible God chose some people and not others. He chose Jacob, but the scriptures say he 'hated Esau.'" Yet, as with the other young adults, he was hesitant to condemn people as non-elect, saying that no one knows who God has not chosen and "it's not our business to judge. As far as we know all can be saved. We know that God is fair and acts in justice. There's a lot we don't know. If you think you've arrived, you probably haven't"

A major difficulty and challenge for the young adults was in observing the Sabbath or the Lord's Day. Unlike many other Christian bodies, most conservative Calvinist churches continue to demand strict restrictions on work and recreation on Sunday. Often the subjects found they had to make sacrifices to observe the Sabbath. This was especially brought home to Ishuwa when she was selected to join a dance company touring Japan. After careful thought and prayer, she decided she could not accept the offer. Her family and friends became angry with her, saying she was throwing her life away. To Ishuwa such reproach is still the hardest part of being Reformed. "It's the way people see you as a fanatic or strange, that you could be doing more with your life." Today she looks forward to the Sabbath. "I find it a blessing not to do what you always do everyday, to spend time with other Christians. And you always feel more ready for the new week." Sabbath observance often caused difficulties in the subjects' families. Today Mark Carbone does not attend family functions and gatherings on Sunday because of his beliefs—a practice that causes considerable tension with his wife and her family. He said observing the Sabbath is like "shaking the dust of the world off for a day. It's resting time. The one day you don't have to battle. When you're at work you are constantly surrounded by unbelievers." Genelli sees the matter in a more pragmatic light. "We were created to rest, its a scientific fact. Why? Because it makes one more productive the rest of the week, and it's one of the commandments."

Submitting To A Community

It was only after interviewing the Reformed young adults that I attended a Sunday morning service at the Orthodox Presbyterian church. As is evident in my interviews so far, the young adults' accounts of their beliefs and practices were very similar to each other, even among those from different congregations. I thought that attending one of their churches might provide more clues in explaining the high degree of uniformity I found among the Reformed. The plain-style structure of the Orthodox Presbyterian church carried no crosses or other religious ornaments, nor did the pastor wear clerical robes. The sanctuary was crowded with people from a wide range of age and racial groups, with young families and crying babies especially prominent; pews in the rear of the church were reserved for families with young children. The service was given over to the reading, reciting, singing and preaching of scripture—both the Old and New Testaments. Instead of standard hymns, the Psalms were sung. The hour-long sermon was based on a detailed, verse-by-verse exposition of a passage from the New Testament.

One of the points the pastor emphasized was that members needed to submit to biblical authority as well as to church leaders and each other in order to keep peace in the church. He said that although members may have personal differences with each other, there should be unity in the church. Such an emphasis on unity generated a strong sense of belonging among the young adults and appeared to influence other areas of their lives. Most of the subjects from the Orthodox Presbyterian church are close friends; in fact, they said that their friends mainly consist of fellow church members. Church Bible studies are usually held at members' homes, thus combining fellowship and friendship with instruction. The subjects from the three churches (Orthodox Presbyterian, independent Reformed and Reformed Baptist) see their fellowships as extended families. All three congregations are experiencing growth in membership.

Christine Ishuwa, a member of an independent Reformed church in New York, said that when she wrote to the pastor seeking information about moving to New York from California to further her dance career, he wrote back saying he could provide her with an apartment. "He didn't even know me! All my friends said, watch out, it's a cult!...But it wasn't a cult. The church has been great. The people are very down-to-earth. It's been like a family to me." When Mark Carbone, a 27-year-old office manager, first visited the Orthodox Presbyterian church he was out of work. "When I told the pastor I was unemployed, he asked me how I was making out financially. I couldn't believe it. The people were concerned."[13] The strong bonds of community at the Orthodox Presbyterian church were demonstrated to Wenzel when his wife had a severe illness needing special treatment in Texas and the church paid for all the expenses.

Most of the subjects said they had few troubles with their churches' teachings and were reluctant to criticize either the Reformed faith or their own congregation. Genelli did say that he is troubled by hypocrisy among some church members and "the feeling that other

Christians may be fakes. Everyone's so nice, you can't tell who's sincere." Charles Dornan faulted Reformed churches for being too entrenched around internal concerns and not committed enough to helping the poor in their neighborhoods. Cynthia Balen was the most critical of fellow Calvinistic believers when she said, "Some Reformed people are very cold. For some reason, the faith has not taken root in [their] lives. For some people, when they learn the doctrines of grace, they get very proud."

A Covenant Community Amidst Evangelical Pluralism

The Calvinist young adults viewed their congregations as a "gathered community" of believers modeling the social and spiritual support that they find in the New Testament. Their journeys to conservative Calvinism usually involved a prior experience with non-Reformed evangelical churches. Much more than their upbringing in Catholicism or mainline Protestantism, the subjects' experience with evangelical churches was decisive in their coming to the Reformed tradition. The Reformed faith was often sharply differentiated from the rest of evangelicalism, with some of these young adults disavowing the "evangelical" label altogether. The list of complaints about mainstream evangelical churches was long: it is shallow, "man-centered," unconcerned with the family (a topic which will be discussed in the next section), ahistorical, overly professionalized, moralistic, secularized, and, most importantly, unbiblical. By "evangelical," the subjects had in mind the diffuse movement typified by a revivalistic heritage based more on personal experience than creeds and confessions.

In their comments about the evangelical world, the young adults had picked up on something that sociologists have only recently begun to study. The pluralism they find rampant within society is also found in varying degrees within the evangelical churches. These young adults would agree with James Davison Hunter in his view that that the younger generation of evangelicals are changing the boundaries of orthodoxy and lack a "consensus on what the Bible teaches about 'basic' points of doctrine (such as the authority of Scripture, the Devil, the origins of the world, Christ's return), about what the family should be, or about the nature of the self and its relevance to Christian living."[14] Hunter writes that the "symbolic boundaries" of Protestant orthodoxy (such as distinctive doctrines and practices that provide a religious identity) "are not being maintained or reinforced" for a number of reasons. Evangelicals are increasingly concerned with tolerance of others and, more importantly, being tolerable to non-evangelicals and not stressing doctrines that may disturb the bonds of civility (such as teachings on hell and judgment). There is also a difficulty among evangelicals believing in the literal truth of doctrines and a tendency to interpret them symbolically (as in the creation accounts in the book of Genesis). The growing pluralism of belief and practice in the evangelical tradition makes such boundary maintenance increasingly difficult.[15]

The young adults' criticisms of evangelicalism are not uncommon among conservative Protestants today. A "confessing" movement has recently emerged among evangelicals largely from conservative Lutheran and Reformed churches that seeks to return to historic Reformation teachings. This group, known as the Alliance of Confessing Evangelicals, has issued a declaration condemning the "pragmatism and consumerism" of the church growth movement and contemporary evangelicals' "dependence upon such modern idols as politics, sociology, marketing and psychology..."[16]

While the young adults were strongly critical of their evangelical counterparts on the same issues which Hunter sees as signaling the changing nature of evangelical orthodoxy, it is worth noting that such criticism was not all out of the standard conservative mold. The evangelical and fundamentalist taboos prohibiting dancing, smoking and drinking also came in for criticism by the young adults for being non-biblical (Hunter finds these taboos fading especially among younger evangelicals). They valued the sense of freedom they found in the Reformed tradition, but also cited the security and stability derived from adhering to a historical body of teachings found in the Reformed confessions of faith. In a sense, the young adults located themselves in a tradition that extended beyond John Calvin and John Knox or even St. Paul, for that matter. The young adults' frequent references to the Old Testament and identification with its teachings on the law and the covenant (as well as their singing of the Psalms in church) provided them with a link to the past, as well as a sense of "choseness" that bears some similarities to Orthodox Jews or even ancient Israel.

For Faith and Family

In the middle of my interview with Bill Wenzel, he balanced his one-year-old daughter on his knee and gave her the cue. "What's the purpose of man?" he asked her. "Glorify God...," gurgled the daughter. "And God is how many?" His daughter held up three fingers and, with her father's coaching, answered, "Three in one." This short lesson from the Westminster Catechism demonstrated more than the daughter's good memory; it shows the high level of importance the subjects place in their families and in transmitting the Reformed faith to them. Almost every young adult was married and had children before they were 30-years-old; the two women, Sally Michael and Christine Ishuwa, who were not married fervently wanted to enter that state. Both women complained that the small numbers of conservative Reformed believers in the New York area provided a small pool of potential mates; they would not consider marrying outside of the Reformed faith unless their spouse would convert to the church. The Reformed doctrine of the covenant, teaching that God includes whole families in the church, (although that does not mean they will all be elected), was emphasized by the subjects to show the importance of the family. [This doctrine is not taught in Reformed Baptist churches, although the subjects from this tradition were equally "pro-family."]

In the Reformed faith "the parents have the number one responsibility to teach their children," Wenzel said. And by "teach," he meant more than religious instruction. All of the young adults plan to either teach their children at home or send them to a Christian school; they often referred to studies showing that students schooled at home are high academic achievers. The Christian school the Orthodox Presbyterian parents have in mind for their children is not run by the church but organized by parents. The public schools were roundly criticized for promoting anti-Christian values, although most parents want to send their children to prestigious secular universities after they receive a rigorous Christian education.

Wenzel added that the "government should not be involved in education. I don't need to have my children getting eight hours of evolution, and then try to undo it every day." His mention of evolution is noteworthy, since the teaching of "creationism," the view that God created humans directly in literal days, played an important role in the subjects' beliefs (and will be discussed in the next section). A stronger use of discipline in childrearing is another practice that the subjects say they have adopted since becoming Reformed. It was a common view that disciplining infants and older children—usually through paddling or spanking—is necessary because everyone is born a sinner. Wenzel said that in his previous evangelical church the prevalent view was that young children were innocent. He was quick to add that one "can't discipline children to anger...The only way to spank a child is with God's rules."

Throughout the interviews, I found a frequent reference to the importance of maintaining a strict hierarchy in the home as taught in the Bible. In this view, the husband is the head of the home, while the wife is to be in submission to him, and the children are to be obedient to their parents. The wives interviewed all stressed that they were called to be "homemakers" as a ministry or a vocation. Thirty-year-old Julie Ferre expressed some wonderment that she moved from her life as a commercial banker to a wife and homemaker today.

> When I was in my early 20s, I would tell my friends that I would never marry, that I didn't want kids. If I wasn't Christian or Reformed, I probably wouldn't have married..But now I'm really enjoying being a helper to my husband. It works beautifully. There's nothing he wouldn't do for me. That's not to say that women can't work. I have nothing against working outside the home. When the children get older, I might want to work at a crisis pregnancy center.

Most of the women subjects showed considerable disdain for feminism. Julie Ferre added that "Feminists tried to say [men and women] are exactly alike and it's a lie. They sold us a bill of goods. There's no room for God in feminism because feminists become their own God." Wenzel's wife, Leslie, was trained as a nurse and continues to study for an advanced degree in that profession. But today she said she has "no desire to advance my career in nursing, because the family is my first ministry."[17]

Among the subjects, only Cynthia Balen, the Reformed Baptist college instructor, said that feminism has had some positive effects for women. "Feminism had its place. Women were being taken advantage of by men. Some women are still underpaid; they deserve the same pay and opportunity as men." Balen said she has "been criticized for having an education and being in business and not having a baby yet, so I suppose I could be considered a feminist...It's like [other Reformed Christians are saying], 'how dare I be so unsubserviant and outshine my husband!'" She said that she chose the education field because she could "drop out to raise kids," (which might involve teaching them at home) and then resume her career when the children are older. Balen stressed, however, that she is critical of much of feminism. "The feminist movement once had a cause, but now they're keeping it going by creating issues that aren't important. It has gotten to the point of being very selfish. There's also more of an attitude of hating men."

When stating their views on marriage, all of the women stressed that they are, in Julie Ferre's words, "perfectly equal" to their husbands, but have different roles to play in the family. The young men were more likely to stress the submission of wives to husbands. But they all emphasized that such a relationship only works in the context of a Christian marriage. All the subjects who were asked about the matter agreed that if the husband abused the wife she would be right to leave him, since he was not exercising his leadership in love and godliness. The view that women should be in submission to their husband sometimes included the concept that women should not exercise leadership roles in society. Again, the men were more likely to take such a position than the women. Genelli said that "History shows that women are great domestically. That's where their fulfillment comes. Look at these single women over 40 who have careers. Do you think they're happy? They're miserable. They act like bitches, they're like hags." Tom Ferre said that men's leadership roles in families and society have become blurred because women have become too powerful. "Men don't sacrifice for things anymore; they're lazy. So women do them because they naturally want to dominate."

The male subjects all agreed that feminism has weakened many men's sense of masculinity, even in the church. Charles Dornan, the Reformed Baptist sales executive, said that Reformed denominations which have considered allowing women into some leadership positions, such as the Christian Reformed Church, are being "feminized." He added that

> Men have the erroneous view that being Christian means being soft and weak. Women do seem more spiritual and many men are afraid what people will say about them [if they become too

religious]. It seems more men are drawn to the Reformed faith because of the male authority you see there. Right now in our church, we're trying to encourage black men to leadership positions, so they can show that not only black women are strong Christians.

An unexpected change in family life and sexuality that developed among some of the couples when they became Reformed was an opposition to artificial birth control. When the ex-Catholic Genelli came to the belief that artificial birth control was wrong, he went to a Catholic parish offering seminars in natural family planning.

> Birth control is unnatural. Some [parents] are saying, 'we want to travel the world,' or 'we just don't want kids.' and I think that's disrupting what God intends in marriage...But you have to be compassionate. If women are having a hard time, or they have problems, I could see exceptions.

Most of the young adults who did oppose artificial birth control— close to half of those interviewed—usually claimed that it violated God's sovereignty. The subjects who did oppose birth control said that Reformed Christians remain divided on this issue, sometimes within the same congregations and families.

Constructing A Christian Worldview

Adjacent to the church offices of the independent Reformed church is a small storefront called the Sabbath School of Dance. At first glance, it did not seem likely that the dance school advertising classes in jazz, ballet and modern dance had any connection with the orthodox Calvinist church next door. Calvinism, after all, has long been associated with a Puritan disdain for pleasure and the body. The young adults did often speak of their faith as governing all their activities and the need to develop a "Christian worldview" on a wide range of issues, but I wasn't sure that would include dance. Christine Ishuwa, the founder and proprietor of the dance school, said confidently that there is no contradictions between her faith and dance. "The Reformed faith is so practical. It encompasses every facet of life."

Ishuwa said her main concern is to teach quality dancing, while also making sure that the school doesn't get too concerned about keeping up with the "world's standard" of dance. "Dancers usually have to sleep, eat and drink dance. But that's wrong. The struggle should be to sleep and eat and drink God." She has also written regulations into the school's bylaws for students and their parents not to take God's name in vain. But more important, Ishuwa is convinced that much of current dance shows a distorted view of sexuality. She is careful, especially with teenagers, not to give them an "over-awareness of their bodies." For this reason, she gives students more modest uniforms in which to train. While recognizing different forms of dance as a "gift from God," she steers students away from "bump and grind" techniques.

Developing a Christian worldview meant different things to different young adults. To most of the Reformed young adults, forming a Christian worldview and lifestyle often concerns matters close at hand: establishing strong Christian families and working hard and honestly; in fact, hard work was one the most cited characteristics of the Christian lifestyle. But when asking them questions about the state of society, their worldviews took on a much broader scope. Anthony Genelli said that "All the news you read, the economics, [and] politics are tied to the will of God. How could they not be when you accept the sovereignty of God? " This belief that current events are part of a grander scheme in God's purposes and that Christians have a grid (the Bible) through which they can detect the threads of meaning and coherence in the world was expressed by all the young adults. Tom Ferre said that his belief that God created the world rather than that it evolved provides a purpose to the world. "If evolution is true, than what Hitler did can be viewed as not too bad, since he felt he was eliminating weaker races, pretty much like getting rid of animals." Society's approval of radical feminism and homosexuality is also traced to an acceptance of evolution, since the theory does not acknowledge God who created differences and natural attraction between males and females.

Most of the subjects have changed their taste in music and entertainment since becoming Reformed. Julie Ferre, once a "deadhead," a fan of the rock band The Grateful Dead, now enjoys mainly hymns. Others reported that they are far more "discerning" in their listening and viewing habits. Almost all of the subjects said they have drastically cut their viewing of television, although they are more likely to watch family-oriented movies on video. Sally Michael said she still likes all types of music and calls contemporary Christian rock music "too schmaltzy." Genelli said he still likes rock, though not the lyrics of many songs. "Some Christians think that rock music is from the pit of hell. They say groups like Iron Maiden and others are anti-God sort of bands. But I think such groups are explaining and describing evil rather than promoting it."

The young adults all believed in the doctrine of "antithesis," teaching that there is an unbridgeable gulf between Christianity and the unbelieving world. Such a view implies that Christians and non-Christians will often have sharply different solutions to society's problems. They were divided as to how much they can change a non-Christian society. Sally Michael and Christine Ishuwa hold to the reconstructionist position that there should be a Christian society run by biblical law and that Christians will bring in the kingdom of God (a view known as postmillenialism). Michael said that a Christian society would limit the state to serving justice, such as administering punishments for crimes, while the church would provide charity and mercy. Most other societal functions, such as education, would be run by families and private organizations. In such a scheme, Michael especially likes the idea that Christian laws would be enforced. "If you don't get one kind of law you'll get another. Wouldn't you want to walk through the streets of New York knowing that there are great Christian laws that would be enforced? Today the only laws that are enforced are parking laws." She favors laws against adultery, abortion, and homosexuality. But she is not sure how such a society would be organized.

Both Ishuwa and Michael believe that such changes will come from the bottom-up, as a growing number of Christians make an impact on society. In the meantime, they are pessimistic about the future of American society and politics in general. Ishuwa said that she does not trust the national government and that "politics is not an honourable calling unless maybe it's in a small town." She said that today

everything is much less Christian than before. It seems that things will get worse before getting better. The world tolerates everything but Christianity; just look at Hollywood...It may be that it's the end of U.S. society, something like the fall of the Roman empire....Everything is becoming more black and white, like the whole thing with AIDS. It's starting to get clearer than one can't

be neutral, can't sit on the fence. You either move away from God
or closer.

Such pessimism was expressed by all the young adults. Dornan said
that while he agrees with the Reconstructionist vision of a Christian-
run society in principal, in reality he sees America becoming less and
less of a Christian country. "You're more likely to see a Christian
society developing in South Korea than in America. Christianity here
is becoming very wishy-washy." Most of the non-reconstructionists
favored a return to biblical laws also, but they did not think this would
hasten or bring in the kingdom of God. Genelli said,

> You can never change the will of man by politics...I favor biblical
> laws, but it doesn't bring in the kingdom. It's true that the country
> was founded on biblical principles. Even our system of
> government with its checks and balances was founded upon
> principles from the Presbyterian church. So even in a corrupt state,
> the country still runs well because we borrowed good ideas.

All of the subjects reported becoming more interested and involved
in politics since becoming Reformed, even if they were pessimistic
about large-scale change. Most of them said they are more likely to
vote since adopting the faith. Such political involvement was largely
based on family issues, such as protests and participation in pro-life
demonstrations and support for school voucher policies. Cynthia Balen
said that her becoming Reformed and Bill Clinton's election to the
presidency both served as factors that drew her into greater political
involvement. She now keeps a file on Clinton and his policies and is
involved in signing and passing around petitions against Clinton's
policies on abortion and health care. Julie Ferre said that she often
writes to politicians on issues such as abortion and gay rights, and has
been strongly involved in pro-life activities since she became
Reformed. "I would like to do more. I think women are really the
victims in abortion."

Unlike some conservative Reformed believers involved in pro-life
efforts using civil disobedience, such as Operation Rescue, the young
adults were against such efforts, citing biblical references against
disobeying the government. "I believe in peaceable demonstrations.
There are so many things to do within the law," Julie Ferre said.
Charles Dornan said he "admires the conviction of the people in

Operation Rescue. My problem with it is whether its helping or hurting [the antiabortion cause]. The way they protest can hurt Christians; it makes them look unwise in the world's eyes." The Reformed young adults often worked with Roman Catholics in pro-life activities, and they reported having few problems with such cooperation. Tom Ferre said that he has met many Catholics whom he now believes are true Christians, although he finds many Catholic teachings unbiblical.

The subjects all supported capital punishment, believing that God mandated such punishment in the Old Testament. All of the subjects said they had no difficulties with interracial dating and marriage. They pointed out that their congregations are multi-ethnic and that such diversity and inclusivity was partly why the faith attracted them. One of the complaints Cynthia Balen leveled against her former non-Calvinistic Baptist church was that it was "too WASPY." She appreciated the greater involvement of blacks in her Reformed Baptist congregation. Tom Wenzel said, "I would much rather my children marry someone outside their race than a non-Christian." When asked what they thought of the growing ethnic and religious pluralism in their neighborhoods, the subjects did not oppose such changes. Ishuwa said she "loves the diversity of New York...The presence of other religions makes us sharp in order to refute other [people's beliefs]. If you have no enemies your sword gets dull." Genelli said he supports "freedom of religion as long as they don't impose [their beliefs] on me."

Yet most of the subjects believed that laws prohibiting work on Sunday and such behavior as adultery and homosexuality should be put into place. They believed strongly that there is a "culture war" between Christians and other with traditional values and non-Christian humanists. Most of the young adults reported listening regularly to popular conservative talk radio host Rush Limbaugh. Although Limbaugh does not make his Christian commitment clear on the air, Julie Ferre said she "appreciates [Limbaugh's] wit and sensitivity. He doesn't put biblical things down, he agrees with a biblical moral standard."

Gay rights was often cited by the young adults to be one of the clearest indicators of such a culture war and the decline of society in general. Homosexuality was seen by Anthony Genelli as a

key issue affecting other issues. Gay rights is a protocol for the
rest of legislation in society...I don't think gays should be
discriminated against, but I don't want them imposing their views
on me. Gays want everyone to accept their way. Today you feel
like you don't have a right to speak out about homosexuality.

He added that he would work to prevent gay rights laws if they
came to his community. Julie Ferre said to promote gay rights is
"wicked. Especially when they ram that garbage down our children's
throats." Charles Dornan said "Homosexuals do not have the right to
live where they want or work where they want when they are
influencing morals or affecting children. They should have rights up to
a point where their lifestyles are not harming people."

The young adults were all equally opposed to the welfare state and
nationalized health care. Often the work ethic they find in the Bible—
if a man doesn't work he should not eat—was cited to defend their
view. There was more support for government programs that would
put those on welfare to work. But most often the church was viewed as
the ideal principal welfare organization—both by reconstructionists
and non-reconstructionists. Tom Ferre said that "the church
abandoned its role of taking care of widows and the poor and the state
took it on, but then abandoned the principle that work is a positive
thing. And that's how things got messed up."

Julie Ferre added that "health care is not a right. It's something
that you get when you work. If you work hard you get rewarded."
Although most of the subjects cautioned that greed and sin can affect
the free market, they strongly supported capitalism. Ferre favors a free
market because "Competition is really good. It helps the
consumer...People who become rich take risks. That's fine, they ought
to be rewarded. I think envy plays a big part in resentment against the
rich...Prosperity can be a blessing from God." Genelli said that
"Anything government goes about doing, it always fails." The attempt
to establish national health care, will "make way for greed, leads to
more litigation, and people trying to get money out of the system. They
say 20 percent are without health care, and that's not bad. Let health
care reform itself." He added that

God's intention for [an economic system] is capitalism. It
encourages competition, and that's good. It creates incentives. If
the rich were not allowed to be rich, then the poor would have no

incentive to work and make money. I want to be rich, because it means I have incentive. Of course, the rich should share with the poor.

Dornan agreed that a "Christian should become as wealthy as he can, as long as he uses the wealth to build up the church and help the poor."

Calvinism As A Weapon In The Culture Wars

As noted earlier, the Reformed young adults uphold doctrines and lifestyles that revive and yet also rearrange the "symbolic boundaries" of orthodox evangelical identity to meet contemporary challenges. Their strong belief in the inerrancy of scripture, creationism, a strong work ethic, and the importance of the family and male-female differences could be seen as attempts to retrieve an evangelical or fundamentalist identity in the face of increasing theological change and uncertainty among many evangelicals. In examining the young adults' accounts, as well as conservative Reformed literature, one finds a fervent reassertion of traditional evangelical teachings that are in contention in the evangelical subculture today. For instance, the role of men and women is in considerable flux in the evangelical world; there is no longer one authoritative position on the ordination of women or whether women are to be submissive or have equal authority in marriage. But in conservative Reformed circles, one finds little uncertainty about such a matter. The idea of women serving as elders or deacons is strictly ruled out, not to mention the ordination of women.

A recent article in a conservative Calvinist magazine echoes the subjects' criticism of the wider evangelical church on such matters. It makes the claim that Christians have "wandered from the Bible's teaching on masculinity." The churches themselves are responsible for the resulting "feminization" of the family and American culture when they began to emphasize the love of Christ (expressed in such hymns as "Softly And Tenderly Jesus Is Calling") and the romantic love of husband for wife in sentimental terms rather than through the Biblical framework of male headship and "unshakable covenantal commitment," according the article.[18] Through such teachings, the young Calvinist men appear to have found a way to reaffirming their masculinity at a time when other men are crowding into stadiums for gatherings of the evangelical men's movement Promise Keepers, or venturing into the woods and the sweat lodges in the same pursuit through other versions of the men's movement. The female subjects' acceptance of homemaking and male headship in marriage was not viewed as making them inferior in marriage. Rather, they claimed to recover their rightful role which they viewed as being equal to that of men. It is worth noting that the women, despite the wide-brush portrayal of feminism as an ungodly movement, were more likely to emphasize equality and open access to most areas of employment, while the male subjects stressed subordination and more limited employment opportunities for women.

The young adults' adoption of conservative Calvinism brought them into a counterculture that served as both a refuge from and a challenge to an increasingly pluralistic society. Other beliefs and practices more directly related to orthodox Calvinism, such as predestination, the importance of biblical law for both individuals and society, Christian schools and home schooling, the freedom from legalistic non-biblical taboos, support for free enterprise and anti-statism, pro-life and anti-gay rights activism, the strict observance of the Sabbath, and the call for a comprehensive Christian worldview, enhance these young adults' evangelical identity with greater resiliancy and distinctiveness in order to withstand and challenge an increasingly pluralistic society. The young adults' belief in predestination and the sovereignty of God provides them with the resources to challenge the trend toward personal autonomy and individualism. Sabbath observance gives these young believers an opportunity to, in Mark Carbone's words, "shake off the dust from the world" after being surrounded by unbelievers all week and recreate a space for Christians not intruded upon by pluralism.

The Calvinists' strong family emphasis that often includes support for home schooling reasserts the primacy of the family in the face of encroaching power by the state into once-private domains (sex education programs being a prime example). As with the Sabbath, the tight-knit conservative Calvinist family serves as an oasis of Christian values in the stormy sea of modern society. The young adults' enthusiasm for capitalism, almost to the degree of libertarianism, and their criticism of statism also plays a similar role in their desire to limit the secularizing influence of government power. Robert

Wuthnow notes that there is a sociological basis for this fear of expanding state power. The sociologist finds that with the significant growth of government in providing social services since World War II, the "relative role played by religion has become much less important." Wuthnow argues that state expansion has had a "significantly negative effect on church membership."[19]

Capitalism is also valued by the young Calvinists as a force for good, providing rewards or "blessings" for their strict work ethic. Their views often read like a page taken from Max Weber's "The Protestant Ethic and the Spirit of Capitalism," which links the development of capitalism with Calvinism, a thesis that more liberal Reformed Christians have long attempted to revise or refute. The conservative Reformed emphasis on the family (including Christian and home schooling) and the biblical vocation of homemaking serve as a stop-gap against the ill-effects of the free market in the home. Social ethicists Don and Carol Browning argue that by "preferring that mothers stay at home and by granting dignity to full-time homemaking, [religious conservatives] block the spread of market values into the inner life of families."[20]

While it is acknowledged that greed can play a role in capitalism, there seemed to be little concern that the free market could also erode many of the values the Calvinist young adults cherish. Capitalism and consumerism can relocate and dislocate families, promote hedonism, and generally disrupt societies attempting to implement biblical principles. Peter Berger writes that modern capitalism is often accompanied by a degree of pluralism which makes any attempt at forming a religious-based based society exceedingly difficult; in communities with growing number of Hindus and Muslims, for instance, it will not be easy to revive blue laws. The growing cultural pluralism in America (evident in the young adults' concern about the entertainment media) is likewise not very amenable to visions of a biblically-based society [It should be noted, however, that the Reformed young adults had little conflict with ethnic pluralism as compared with cultural pluralism; they were likely to cite the racial openness of their congregations in their accounts, taking pride in the fact that they embraced all races]. The financial prosperity that the Reformed believer claims as the reward for hard work and virtue can also fall into the hands of amoral media magnates and complacent stock investors. As Berger writes, "The market rewards and punishes individuals impersonally, without regard to the moral qualities that allegedly distinguish them."[21]

It can be argued that the above positions are not necessarily what John Calvin and subsequent Reformed theologians had in mind when they proposed and elucidated the "doctrines of grace." The young adults' stress on the inerrancy of scripture, for instance, was not a central part of the theology of Calvin. Nor is the countercultural thrust of the young adults' social outlook one that is shared by many Reformed thinkers throughout history. The subjects have retrieved and reformulated elements from the Reformed tradition which best provide authoritative "answers" to the overriding realities of society they have faced as young adults, such as individualism, secularism, and, most of all, pluralism and the resulting fragmentation of life.

The young adults' often bleak portrayals of the threats of secularism and unbelief in the wider society and in other churches may well be exaggerations but they are of use in fortifying their religious identity in the face of such pluralism. The conservative Reformed doctrine of "antithesis" also served to highlight the degree of conflict in which they see themselves with society, setting up an "us-against the world" scenario. Calvinism has often been considered to be a tradition that has pressed for the transformation rather than for withdrawal and sharp conflict with culture. The young adults did not disavow the concept of transforming society, but they recognized the difficulty of such a project in today's pluralistic society, especially through using legal measures. The recognition that one can change a culture and society without pressing for Christian laws could be glimpsed in the subjects' advocacy of private and home-schooling, as well as in Christine Ishuwa's determined attempt to "reform" dance according to biblical standards. The young adults' "countercultural" concerns with the family, hard work, private schooling, and the blessings of the free market can in fact play a significant role in American society. The Republican resurgence of 1994 suggests that such concerns can quickly become part of the political and cultural landscape, although such a change will not necessarily increase conservative Christian influence on society.

These young adults, including the Reconstructionists who have an optimistic theology of world transformation, seemed resigned to the view that American society is in decline. There was little mention by the subjects of the Calvinist concept of "common grace," the view that

God can work through people, institutions and religions that are not Reformed or even Christian. Most of these young adults' concerns turn on more immediate, local-based concerns: the health and structure of their families, finding a mate, the local congregation, and the hard work they put into their careers. The exceptions to such private concerns can be found in their involvement in the pro-life movement and in their attempts to stop gay rights and other "anti-family" measures. For these Calvinists, fighting for such issues are an effort to protect their piece of turf in a society undergoing a "culture war," a protracted battle between what they see as Christian and non-Christian worldviews. It is no coincidence that James Davison Hunter profiled an Orthodox Presbyterian pastor fighting the gay rights movement in San Francisco as his case study for "orthodox" believers in his 1991 book "Culture Wars." These young adult Calvinists are living on the front lines of such a conflict.

CHAPTER 3:

Eastern Orthodoxy

Eastern Orthodoxy has been called a sleeper on the American religious scene. Although Orthodox churches have a combined membership of approximately 3 million believers in the U.S., the visibility and influence of this religious tradition in American society in the recent past has been marginal. On first impression, Eastern Orthodoxy does not appear to be a religion that would attract many Americans, either young or old. The churches take pride in maintaining millennium-old traditions and teachings from foreign cultures, while Americans change and reformulate beliefs and theology from one decade to the next. Orthodox churches have an authority-based nature, emphasizing confession and spiritual oversight by a priest and requiring rigorous disciplines such as fasting. The tradition also has a vibrant mystical component. A typical Orthodox service with its rich liturgical traditions of chanting and prayers and adoration of icons can extend past two hours. American religious instincts, on the other hand, have often been strongly individualistic and pragmatic, often adapting institutions to meeting individual needs. Orthodox scholars are still debating whether there can be an "American Orthodoxy."

Orthodoxy is still often seen as an ethnic and exotic religion that has yet to plant its roots in America. While it is true that many Orthodox churches maintain connections to their "mother" countries, such as Russia and Greece, the members of these bodies have become increasingly assimilated into American society. The assimilation of Orthodox Americans has in some cases meant that such Americans have left their Orthodoxy behind. Such a Slavic-based denomination as the Orthodox Church in America (with an official membership estimate of one million) is about half as large as it was 30 years ago, as the children and grandchildren of ethnic members have intermarried and dropped out of the church, according to Orthodox theologian Thomas Hopko. He writes that in the 1950s, sociologists of religion were already predicting such steep declines because Orthodox churches were too divided (often along ethnic lines), with a lack of central authority.[1]

The highly ethnic Greek Orthodox Church, the largest Orthodox body in the U.S., has yet to lose a large number of its members, although some observers see such a process just beginning to take place as second and third generation members lose their immigrant loyalty to the church through assimilation and intermarriage. The dropout rate in Eastern Orthodoxy may be more dramatic than even its own leaders have claimed. In a City University of New York survey of religious identity, it was estimated that the actual Orthodox population is closer to 0.5 million adults, suggesting that many of the baptized members counted by officials no longer identify with the tradition. CUNY researchers Barry Kosmin and Seymour Lachman conclude that the newer figure may show that this "ethnic, ceremonial-focused religion is losing touch with the younger generations of North Americans."[2]

In the past 10 years, however, there has been an unexpected turn of events. A slow yet steady stream of converts have been making their way into Orthodoxy. The converts have come from a wide variety of backgrounds and perspectives, including former evangelical Protestants, high church Episcopalians, Roman Catholics, mainline Protestants, followers of New Age spirituality, and those with no previous faith. The reasons given for such conversions are as numerous as the different kinds of people attracted to the faith. Ex-evangelicals say they are finding an ancient source of spirituality and a sense of tradition; former Anglicans (who have converted in the greatest numbers) and other mainline Protestants find a firmer base of doctrinal and ecclesial authority; former Catholics value Orthodoxy's decentralized leadership structure and its preservation of spiritual disciplines that are no longer in place in many parishes since the modernizing influence of Vatican II.

The influence of converts is evident throughout Orthodoxy. The majority of the 12 bishops of the Orthodox Church in America are converts from non-Orthodox backgrounds. For the past several years, about 40 percent of the seminarians at the OCA's St. Vladimir's Seminary in Crestwood, N.Y. have been converts. The most dramatic examples of conversion to Orthodoxy took place in the late 1980s. In 1987, a group of 2,400 Christians with its origins in the evangelical Campus Crusade for Christ made news when it joined en masse the Antiochian Orthodox Archdiocese. In 1989, the San Francisco-based Christ the Savior Brotherhood, a 1000-member communal group with its roots in a mystical New Age movement (known as the Holy Order of Mans) from the 1960s, was received into Orthodoxy.[3] More recently, congregations from a diversity of backgrounds—from Anglican to independent charismatic—have been converting to Orthodoxy. Baby boomers and younger believers appear to comprise the "lion's share" of conversions to Orthodoxy, according to Fr. Peter Gillquist, director of evangelism and missions in the Antiochian Orthodox Archdiocese. In fact, the new wave of converts to Orthodoxy has been described, and derided by critics, as "Orthodox baby boomers." In talks to groups of converts and prospective converts around the U.S., Gillquist finds a growing interest in Orthodoxy among college students.[4]

It remains to be seen whether or not this movement of converts will replenish the ranks of Orthodoxy after many of its ethnic members have departed. It is clear, however, that Orthodoxy is being reshaped by these newcomers, as well as by the continuing process of assimilation. Such converts as Gillquist and Frank Schaeffer (who is the son of prominent evangelical philosopher Francis Schaeffer) have retained their evangelical preaching style as they have toured the nation calling for Orthodox renewal and conversion. That some of these converts have retained an evangelical concern to argue and prove the "truth" of Orthodoxy from the Bible has been a source of concern among Orthodox theologians. English is becoming the common language in most Orthodox parishes. Parishes that have welcomed a large number of converts have reported a greater degree of parishioner participation in the liturgy, such as in singing the hymns and chants traditionally reserved for the choir.[5] Orthodox texts on spirituality are now widely being translated into English and distributed in the U.S. A spate of new periodicals, often founded and edited by converts, have appeared attempting to bring Orthodox perspectives on modern society, such as the *Saint Sophia Quarterly*, *The Christian Activist*,

Again, *Epiphany* and *Axios*. Eastern Orthodoxy is also coming into greater contact with other religious traditions—both through ecumenical activity and, in some quarters, activism on pro-life issues. Such converts as Schaeffer and Frances Matthewes-Green have been in the forefront of pro-life activism.

There has also been a steady movement of young adults returning to the Orthodox churches of their birth, especially the Greek Orthodox Church. It is estimated that 50 to 75 percent of Greek Orthodox young people drop out of parish life during college years and in their 20s. As such disaffected Greek Orthodox young adults reach their late 20s and 30s, approximately 30 to 50 percent return to active parish life. Such a pattern of return is not only a matter of married young adults returning to the church of their youth to raise their children, since many of such returnees are single. The Greek Orthodox young people's motivations for coming back to the church revolve largely around spiritual concerns rather than ethnic ones.[6]

The following case studies of Orthodox young adults were conducted with members from several Orthodox bodies. The subjects include both converts and ethnic members who have returned to the church during young adulthood. Six of the ten subjects belonged to the Orthodox Church in America. The other subjects belonged to the Russian Orthodox Church Abroad, the Greek Orthodox Archdiocese of North and South America, and the Carpatho-Russian Orthodox Greek Catholic Church. These Orthodox jurisdictions are united on most points of doctrine and practice, although the Russian Orthodox Church Abroad follows the old calendar for the church year and has little association with other Orthodox bodies.

Walking On To A Different Planet

My interview with Mariame Javic took place while she was running the thrift shop at her Orthodox parish for the day. In the middle of her responses she would sometimes jump from her seat to bargain with customers and then return to the interview without losing her train of thought. With her Slavic accent, long dress, and veil on her head, it wasn't difficult to think of Javic as a traditional ethnic Orthodox young woman at the marketplace. But like the other Orthodox subjects I was soon to interview, the 32-year-old filmmaker was a mixture of the traditional and modern. A few weeks later, in more stylish clothes and with a cigarette often dangling between her fingers, Javic showed me a sampling of her films. The clips she showed me depicted New York buildings and street life through off-center camera angles using rap and jazz soundtracks. Javic jokingly referred to the more abstract works as representing her "pre-Orthodox life." But it seemed that she was able to strike a delicate balance between her "downtown" New York sensibility and work and her Orthodox faith.

Mariame Javic was baptized a Catholic in Eastern Europe but said that religion played little role in her or her family's life. When she was 23 she came to New York to study filmmaking. Javic gradually gained a reputation in the film world for her work and considered herself successful. She frequented nightclubs and parties but often felt unhappy, "that life was useless." She said she felt "dead...unable to find fulfillment." She was also getting tired of the money-oriented film and art culture of New York. During this time, she would often visit a friend who was an iconographer at a small Orthodox parish in Brooklyn. "He was so honest and understanding; it was a refuge going to the church and talking with him." While visiting her friend about three years ago, Javic decided to attend a service at the church.

> It was like I walked on to a different planet. At first, I was curious. Then I started to smell the incense and [began] feeling very self-conscious. It was like I could only see myself and my sins, but could not see anything else. I almost felt like I was going to faint and I ran out of the church as soon as the service was over.

But Javic was struck by the ornate beauty and holiness she found in the church, especially the icons. She began to feel that she had to make changes in her life. "I went to every vesper service at the church after that. I began to enter a process of change." She now often uses the name by which she was chrismated (or confirmed), and has adopted a simple lifestyle, eschewing her former ambitions of wealth and success. In her filmwork, she now tries to portray themes and images that are "positive" and beneficial, such as concern for the environment and the poor, as well as draw artistic inspiration from icons.[7]

Reading Their Way Into The Faith

As I began interviewing Eastern Orthodox young adults in their homes, I expected I would encounter the exotic atmosphere one associates with Eastern Christianity—colorful icons, strange scents, strains of ethnic music, and perhaps even long-bearded men and scarved women. Several male subjects did have beards and Javic did wear that veil (although only on special church occasions), but there was little else that distinguished the Orthodox young adults from other people in their outward appearance. The subjects appeared to be ordinary people who converted or returned to Orthodoxy through a good deal of study and searching. The bookshelves and tables of their homes and churches were often filled with pamphlets and books explaining the faith in clear, straight-forward terms. "You'll find that many of the converts have read their way into the faith," one member of an Orthodox parish told me when I first inquired about interviewing young converts. I have to admit, I never thought of the Orthodox, with their icons and incense, as people of the Book, let alone books.

My prejudices were further disturbed when I met Simeon Baumann, an intense-looking 27-year-old teacher with a long beard, at his book-lined lower Manhattan apartment. He was raised in a devout Roman Catholic home, but it was during his adolescence that he fully embraced the faith "almost overnight...I was attracted to the human element of the church, of Christ's love for humanity." During this time he also considered taking a vow for religious life in the church and started investigating different orders. During college, Baumann was particularly drawn to the Jesuits for their tradition of disciplined prayer and intellectual acumen. But when he actually began associating with a group of Jesuits, he found their concerns more worldly than spiritual. "They were bitter, scheming people. They often stabbed each other in the back and were more concerned about what dining hall to eat at than prayer." Although the Jesuits spoke much about their traditional Ignatian spiritual exercises, Baumann said he did not see any "positive spiritual charism" [or spiritual gift] among them.

After deciding not to pursue a religious vocation, Baumann went to study at a divinity school, where he took courses on liturgy. It was during this time that he started reading such Eastern Orthodox theologians as John Meyendorff and Alexander Schmemann.

> I wanted to learn how to pray and these books were helpful. But I also thought that there was Orthodox rhetoric and then there would be the Orthodox reality, like with the Jesuits. After I attended my first Orthodox liturgy, I was pleasantly surprised, even enthusiastic...It was the feeling that I found something that should have existed.

He started attending an Orthodox Church in America (OCA) parish in Brooklyn, but encountered difficulties with his girlfriend, a Catholic convert. "She said the service was too foreign to her. I thought it was foreign too; it was foreign to the secularization that has crept into Western culture. Orthodoxy is intended to confront you as foreign." Baumann tried to find a Catholic parish to attend for the sake of the relationship, but found himself "more and more frustrated with parishes based around 12-step programs and being against abortion— things that didn't have anything to do with worship at all." He began to become increasingly depressed and felt that his faith was in crisis. "I was at the point where I could not identify anything that was religious in what I did, how I lived." His relationship with his girlfriend broke off during this period. After a trip to Europe, he returned to the Orthodox parish in Brooklyn and was received into the faith a year ago. "It saved my life. I felt very much at home and welcomed," he said. Baumann added that if the "Western [Roman Catholic] church had kept its liturgical integrity more faithfully, I would have stayed. Becoming Orthodox was not a matter of forsaking the papacy or anything like that."[8]

Robin Genovese, a 28-year-old graduate student and instructor in American literature, discovered Orthodoxy through books and a personal search for the right church. She was raised in a "typical secular humanist New York family," with a Jewish mother and an unchurched Italian-American father. She never went to church or synagogue and celebrated both Passover and Christmas. When she was young she started reading the Bible as literature and found it fascinating. She would often devour the books in the religion sections of libraries. When she entered college, she found herself "wishing to believe" in Christianity, and started attending different churches, while continuing to read about different faiths, including Eastern Orthodoxy. During this process of searching, the Orthodox church stood out from the other churches. In looking for a church she said her biggest anxiety was having my individuality absorbed into a religious community. I felt very constrained in other churches. It was so important to be part of a religious community. With the Orthodox church the only reason to be there was worship. I didn't have my individuality threatened by social standards....In attending all of the other churches, I never felt I was able to breathe. In Orthodoxy, I was able to breathe[9]

Forming A Spiritual Community

While a good deal of independent reading and searching drew many of the young adults to the Orthodox church, it was the liturgy and the spiritual disciplines of the faith that kept them there. The emphasis on spirituality was often cited as Orthodoxy's most appealing feature. Mariame Javic said she values the "timelessness of Orthodoxy, the whole cycle of the liturgy and the mysticism of it. It's very original, very pure." She, as well as most of the other subjects, frequently prays the "Jesus Prayer," a brief petition ("Lord Jesus have mercy on me a sinner") intended to bring awareness of God's presence throughout the day.

Baumann sees the liturgy as "organically linking private prayer with public prayer." Baumann said he can't conceive of his life without prayer. "Before when I didn't pray, I would feel guilty. But now when I forget to pray, I feel bad because I am aware of neglecting my soul." When Baumann was a Catholic, his prayers were informal and personal rather than formal (or read from a prayer book) and his fasting was more self-determined and undisciplined. The required Orthodox disciplines of regular fasting, formal prayers, and confession provides the sense that "you're not doing it alone. The people from my own community are doing it, and that [sense of communal devotion] becomes a part of me."

Similar views on the communal nature of such spiritual disciplines as fasting, formal prayers, and spiritual readings, were expressed by Jill Cook, a 29-year-old graduate student in theology. Cook had converted to Christianity through the Episcopal Church while she was a college student in the South. In moving to Boston after graduation, she sought a parish that emphasized prayer and spirituality. But she found the Episcopalians there polarized between liberal parishes focusing mainly on social action and "Anglo-Catholics with English accents who opposed women priests—things that weren't part of my agenda." Cook found a "Gospel and prayer-based community" in an Episcopal monastery, and she gradually began to live a "semi-monastic" lifestyle based around prayer and spiritual readings. It was around this time that she attended an Eastern Orthodox church, mainly out of curiosity. "I immediately felt at home...There was the internal sense that prayer was going on here." As an Orthodox Christian she values the rule of morning and evening prayers as well as fasting

> because it's part of the church discipline. Before [as an Episcopalian], I felt like this lone spiritual athlete. It was voluntary and I had all these standards I set for myself. Now there's just this ordinariness about being Orthodox; I'm just part of the community.

Cook and several other converts drew a connection between childhood and adolescent experiences and their attraction to and eventual adoption of Orthodoxy. As a youth, Cook said she was more introspective than her contemporaries, preferring to "live in a fantasy world," through reading such books as J.R. Tolkien's trilogy, "The Hobbit," rather than going out and playing sports. Although Cook went to a Baptist church only occasionally with her grandfather, by adolescence she had developed an abiding interest in spirituality. On one occasion she tried to "create a kind of liturgical life" by building a shrine to a nearby lake. Although Cook said that such yearnings were "pantheistic," they were an attempt to connect an "awe of nature and the material with a spiritual life"—a desire for which she found fulfillment in Orthodoxy.[10]

Wendy Kent, a 26-year-old graduate student and former Episcopalian, said she "always remembers being interested in liturgy." Her father was a priest in the "high church" or Anglo-Catholic tradition of the Episcopal Church and he would sometimes take her to Orthodox liturgies and weddings. When she would imagine her own wedding as a child, it would often involve the crowning of the bride and groom that takes place at Orthodox weddings. As with Jill Cook, she said that she always had an interest in creation and how it relates to spirituality. Kent was drawn to Orthodoxy while a junior in college because its liturgy brought together the physical and the spiritual.

"Your whole body is involved. It's not like your mind is away somewhere. In the liturgy you're always bowing, prostrating yourself, crossing yourself, kissing icons. It's wholistic."[11]

The subjects all had close ties to their parishes, in some cases traveling long distances to attend services. The parish of the Orthodox Church in America that drew Baumann into its membership is led by a young priest who is enthusiastic about sharing Orthodoxy with those outside of its traditional ethnic boundaries. About 40 percent of the growing parish consists of converts. The sense of welcome and community that these young adults find at the church is repaid through their continued devotion to parish life. Baumann said that before he moved to Orthodoxy he felt that "all the energy I had invested in the church was not of service to anyone." When he came to the Orthodox church, he had the sense that "here was a place where I could invest my energy and it wouldn't be wasted." Several of the subjects attend up to four services a week at their parishes.

Without any prompting from my part, most of the young adults mentioned the psychological benefits of their Orthodox practices and disciplines. Jeff Rogoff, a 32-year-old musician, was baptized as an infant into the Russian Orthodox Church Abroad (a strongly traditional body which broke ranks with the Russian Orthodox Church during the Russian Revolution). He became distant from the church during his teen years, saying the services felt "foreign" to him. In his early 20s he developed a manic depressive illness that led him to search for spiritual solace and healing in a variety of churches—from Pentecostal to Lutheran. After a year of searching, he started to attend an Eastern Orthodox parish. "I felt I arrived back where I should have been all along." He said the other churches were "too different" and that the "purity" of the Orthodox liturgy and the disciplines of prayer, fasting, and spiritual readings help provide order to a sometimes emotionally erractic life.[12]

Mariame Javic said that since she has been in the church and practiced its spiritual disciplines she has been more able to concentrate on her work and other activities, such as reading. The habit of prayer, such as in saying the Jesus Prayer, helps her focus her mind and avoid distractions. She added that such practices as fasting "are tools for fighting the passions. When you can do anything, you lose interest in things. But when you put a limit on what you can do and sometimes stop doing them [such as during fasts], it really makes you enjoy things more." She added that her life in the church has changed how she relates to people.

> Before I always thought I was better than other people. I was very competitive and I despised those who were weak. When I came to the church, I really started to love people. In coming to church and finding guidance and developing a prayer life, I often feel like I'm returning back to a feeling I had when I was a child, a kind of pure joy.

Javic said that Orthodoxy teaches that the soul is connected to the body and mind of a person. When the soul is nourished through such spiritual disciplines, it also has an affect on the other components of a person. She finds that the mysticism of Orthodoxy is close to that of Buddhism. Wendy Kent said that when she first went to an Orthodox vespers service during college, she recalls hearing a chanted prayer calling for the healing of evil memories. "I thought that was so cool to pray for something like that. I also remember thinking, 'Wow, that's healthy.' I had been through a 12-step program and that was a major emphasis there." Robin Genovese said her faith helped her overcome fears of the unknown she had experienced in her childhood and adolescence and has given her greater confidence.

Of course, the spiritual value of the Orthodox disciplines was also mentioned by the young adults. Genovese said fasting was important because "We eat all the time. So by fasting whenever we're hungry we are reminded of what life is about, it reminds you of God. It serves to make you leaner, more disciplined. It invokes a seriousness that is very valuable." When Jeff Rogoff returned to Orthodoxy, he developed close ties with the priest of a nearby parish, viewing him as his father and counselor in the faith. "I go to the psychiatrist for help with my mental illness, but the help I get from my priest on spiritual issues I can't get anywhere else." Such a one-on-one mentoring relationship is often combined with confession, a practice that most of the subjects valued for providing a support system and initiation process into their new or recovered faith. [It should be noted that the subjects' spiritual father or confessor was not always their parish priest.]

Jill Cook said that this relationship with her priest has been "very important. Not being a person who really had a father's guidance growing up, spiritual fatherhood has been very important to me, very healing of my relationship with men, as well as women." The subjects also praised the non-rigid approach taken in confession. Kent said that the

> church doesn't take this cut-and-dry approach to things. While it has very traditional rules, it takes a very organic approach to life. The rules [such as on fasting and prayers] are like guidelines, but you're not belittled if you can't live up to them. It's like my priest says, 'the rules are made to be broken.'

If the priest served as a mentor, the subjects' fellow Orthodox believers often served as role models and encouragers in the faith. When she was considering converting to Orthodoxy, it was an Orthodox friend who convinced Genovese that one could be "young, smart, and cool and still be a Christian." Simeon Baumann said that he "immediately respected and wanted to be like" the people he met at his new church. "They were what I was looking for in the Jesuits—a people formed by grace."

As might be expected, the recent converts were the most religiously active and the least critical of Orthodoxy and their parishes. Those involved in the church longer reported more struggles with the institutional and everyday realities of Orthodoxy. Genovese said that in her eight years in Orthodoxy she has spent months away from her parish and says she is always questioning her "faith, myself and God." Her struggle often extends to her life in the church. After college she became a regular member of an Orthodox Church in America parish in New York. Gradually she became part of the church community, but such a sense of belonging has had its drawbacks.

> I know that believing in God means being in the church. But the church is a lot like being in a giant family. You get a lot of support and you get a lot of blame; there's gossip and bickering like everywhere else. It's this thing of my being an individualist and rubbing up against the institution...There's pressure to conform to certain standards.

The conflict had been brought home to Genovese in her plans for her upcoming marriage. She is marrying a non-Orthodox man who has not been baptized (although he is a Christian), making it unallowable for her to have an Orthodox wedding. "I know I'm doing the right thing. But there is the anxiety of not meeting up to the canon [church law]." When I asked Genovese how Orthodoxy has affected her lifestyle and values, she replied that the "church serves more as a reminder of what my values have always been."

In the Manhattan office where she works as a political consultant, 32-year-old Susan Miller keeps an icon of Jesus over a desk cluttered with pages of polling data. She admitted that there is an "unresolved" relationship between her faith and a career where she consults for a wide range of political groups on causes, some of which she has had disagreements; her work with the tobacco industry was one such recent example. "My beliefs as a Christian should make me more considerate about how I use my talents in the workplace." She added that the church has not always helped her meet the challenges of the modern world.

> There's a tendency for some Orthodox people to wish they were in another time and place. They might say, 'If only this was 19th century Russia,' or 'If only we were all Orthodox.' It's very explicitly a rejection of the modern world...a kind of ghettoization of the faith.

Miller often finds a similar attitude among new converts. "They artificially impose certain things on themselves that can be very negative. It seems that they're denying certain parts of themselves. Ultimately they return to being more themselves." Miller and several other subjects also said that the divisions and "politics" played within and between the various Orthodox churches troubled them. Miller said she sometimes has to "reread books on Orthodoxy to remind myself why I am Orthodox."[13]

Spirituality Versus Ethnic Roots

The ethnic element in Orthodoxy was also seen as a point of conflict for several subjects, including the ethnic Orthodox young adults themselves. Susan Miller said that although she has been Orthodox for more than half of her lifetime, she is still seen as convert "because I'm not Russian or Greek." She added that the ethnic dimension of the faith "acknowledges the good things in these cultures. But at the same time, it can be something that contributes to the marginalization of the faith. You know, people can dismiss it as something that's just that Greek thing." Robin Genovese said that the stress put on ethnicity in some Orthodox churches can be "very annoying. I'm Jewish and Italian and I feel a strong attachment to my own background, so I sometimes feel left out." Simeon Baumann viewed the ethnic factor in a more positive light than the other converts. He said in his parish he appreciates the way "cultures are redeemed and celebrated—Russian, Greek, Yugoslavian. I never feel excluded but welcomed. The ethnic element is not hidden...People are more interested in sharing the positive aspects of their cultures."

Even the Orthodox subjects born into the faith did not make a strong connection between Orthodoxy and their ethnicity. Jeff Rogoff, who is a member of a strongly traditional Russian Orthodox body, said that his return to Orthodoxy "had nothing to do with" his Russian ethnic background. "My return to the Russian Orthodox Church was more of a coming full circle back to where I started. It seems people are coming to the church for its theology more than its ethnic heritage."

For John Gaglias, a 28-year-old waiter at a Long Island diner, the link between his Greek ethnic background and Orthodoxy has become less important as he has moved deeper into the faith. His parents, who are from Greece, brought him regularly to services in the Greek Orthodox Church. In high school he became distanced from the church and only went to services on feast days to please his parents. When he was in college studying engineering, he attended a business seminar where the speaker claimed that he became rich because God was helping him. The idea caught his attention. "It was strange. He was talking about God and money; I couldn't make the correlation. But he also told us to return to our own churches and look for God there." Gaglias went back to his home parish where he encountered a young priest who preached relevant sermons and welcomed questioners. He formed a close relationship to this priest, who eventually became his father confessor.

He started attending a Greek Orthodox young adult organization that put a heavy emphasis on spirituality and evangelism. Yet he often experienced doubts about the truth of his faith during this time and was considering attending other Christian churches. He would often shoot a barrage of questions at priests about the faith. "I think like an engineer; I want to put the pieces together and see how it works. When I saw these priests so strong in the faith, it made me want to know how they got like that." This period of uncertainty, which lasted about three years, ended when he came across a book called "Becoming Orthodox," by Peter Gillquist, a former evangelical Protestant leader who converted to Orthodoxy. "Gillquist traced the origins of the church back to Christ. He presented just the facts. It was a matter of going back into the past and comparing it with the Bible. The book gave me concrete evidence of the truth of Orthodoxy. It solidified everything." He also became more convinced in his faith through reading about miracles occurring in Orthodoxy, such as the weeping icons of the Virgin Mary.

Today, Gaglias is taking a home correspondence course in Orthodox theology from a new Orthodox academy affiliated with Gillquist (which is not connected with Greek Orthodoxy) and is considering becoming a theology teacher. He said that when he returned to the faith he was "turned off by the ethnicity of the church." While he now appreciates the Orthodox heritage of his Greek ancestry, he also feels that ethnicity in the church is often abused, mostly by parishioners who stress their Greek backgrounds to the detriment of spirituality. Today many of his associations are with non-Greek Orthodox groups. His main criterion for finding a wife is that she be devoutly Orthodox; Greek ethnicity is of little importance.[14]

Aileen Koulis, a 33-year-old engineer from Westchester County, is also from a Greek background. She was raised in Greek Orthodoxy and attended church fairly regularly until her early teen years. Her whole family became less active in the church as time went on, only attending on holidays. When Koulis was 20 she went to college in California. It was during this time that she developed a close tie to a Greek Orthodox priest whom she met at a wedding. "He took a real interest in me. I started attending church and I had the feeling that I was where I was supposed to be." She became active in the Orthodox parish, working with young people and serving on the parish council. Koulis said that today when she goes to church, "I feel like I'm leaving the world behind. Attending the liturgy gives me the strength for the rest of the week."

In looking back on her return to the church, Koulis said that it was providential she made the move to California.

> I wasn't the type of person to break away from my family like that. But If I stayed home, with the influence of my father [who was not active in the Greek Orthodox Church], I probably wouldn't have

came back to the church. In California I was able to question a lot of things on my own.

While Koulis is an active member of a Greek Orthodox parish, today she also attends liturgies of the non-ethnic Orthodox Church in America. Koulis said that "Greekness doesn't have much of a role" in her faith. A recent trip to the mission field in Uganda, where she experienced the Orthodox liturgy in a different culture and language, has confirmed her belief that "there's a universality to the [faith]. Orthodoxy is a religion for everybody."[15]

Peter Rensky was the only subject who made strong connections between his faith and ethnicity—and he is a convert. Rensky, a 26-year-old clerk for a financial firm on Wall Street, was baptized in the Eastern Rite Catholic church (which accepts the papacy) and raised as an Episcopalian until he dropped out of church in high school. His grandparents came from the Carpathian mountains in present day Slovakia, a region that was once largely Eastern Orthodox but under force became Eastern-Rite Catholic in the 16th century. In America his family was of mixed religious background, including Episcopalian, Eastern-Rite Catholic, and Orthodox. When he was living in Poland as a student he began looking into his family background and started attending an Orthodox church. When he met his prospective wife, a Bulgarian women of Orthodox background, the decision to become Orthodox was settled for him. "I tried attending the Catholic church but I never felt at home or comfortable there. The Orthodox Church reflected what the Christian church should be, especially because it remained very conservative and centered on traditional values." Rensky had been troubled by the increasing liberalization in the Episcopal Church in the U.S., particularly over the issues of women priests and homosexuality.

The need to find his roots was impressed upon Rensky when he lived in California several years ago.

> The people there are very lost as to where they came from. That's why you see a lot of people looking at exotic religions like Buddhism. I wouldn't go so far as to say it's biological, but there is a link between ethnic background and spirituality. The familiarity that you get [about a faith] from grandparents and parents is important in establishing a spiritual identity.

Rensky now belongs to a parish of the Carpatho-Russian Orthodox Greek Catholic Church, a small Orthodox body based in Pennsylvania. While he said he has no difficulties accepting the many non-Carpatho-Russians who attend the parish, he is troubled that non-ethnic Orthodox sometimes want to eliminate the ethnic identity of the parish. "If they want a strictly American Orthodoxy, let them go to the Orthodox Church in America. The people who come into the church should recognize that it's ethnic. There's no reason to obliterate its identity." Rensky was less religiously observant (such as in observing the fasts and attendance of the liturgy) than the other subjects, which he attributed to his long working hours. While he still retains most of his old friends, he has formed new friendships based more on common ethnic ties (which would include Eastern-rite Catholics) than on a common Orthodox faith.[16]

It is evident that the older connections between Orthodoxy and ethnicity and cultural identity were not strongly felt among most of the young adults. These young adults' Orthodox affiliations were based largely on individual choice and spiritual priorities. Such attitudes mirror the decreasing importance of ethnicity in most American Orthodox bodies. This process of assimilation is now taking place in Greek Orthodoxy but less so within such smaller bodies as the Carpatho-Russian Church. Greek Orthodox young adult official Angelo Ardemaz said that many of the young adults who are second and third generation Greek- Americans drop out in the first place because "all they're finding is ethnicity in their parishes." When these young adults return to the faith, they tend to downplay the Greek ethnic element of the Orthodox faith.[17] Increasingly, Greek Orthodox churches are using mainly English in their services, especially outside of ethnic communities. It is likely that such young returnees as Koulos and Gaglias will accelerate the process of Americanization in Greek Orthodoxy.

A vignette of the changing views of the relation of ethnicity to faith is suggested in Rensky's and Koulis' accounts of their move to Orthodoxy. Rensky's experience of living in California made him critical of the lack of roots among people in this part of the U.S. His stay in such an "uprooted" culture convinced him of the importance of knowing where one comes from and how belief is linked to family and ethnic background. Yet, the fact that Peter Rensky's most recent friends are more likely to be fellow ethnics, including Roman Catholic

Carpatho-Russians, rather than Orthodox Christians of other backgrounds suggests that his concern with ethnicity is not strictly a byproduct of Orthodox faith. Koulis, on the other hand, claimed that leaving her ethnic family with their nominal, ethnic-based religiosity behind and moving to California had actually given her the freedom to explore and then embrace Orthodoxy. She arrived at the Orthodox destination through self-exploration and questioning—the same "Californian" characteristics which Rensky viewed as being so damaging to tradition and a sense of belonging.

Different Visions of the Church.

So far, the accounts of belief and practice among Eastern Orthodox young adults that I heard in the interviews did not form a very neat pattern. Orthodoxy is a complex and many-layered tradition and the subjects were a diverse group about whom it is difficult to make many generalizations. Just when I often thought I could pinpoint a common tendency of thought among most of the young adults, there were usually several exceptions that would break the rules. Eventually I came to the conclusion that the pluralism among the subjects forms a significant pattern in itself in understanding young adult conversion and return to Orthodoxy. This diversity is evident in the various ways the subjects have adopted and then adapted Orthodoxy to their lives.

When John Gaglias returned to his parish he was more concerned about finding "concrete evidence" from history on the truth of Orthodoxy (and convincing others of such truths) than in returning to his Greek spiritual roots. Peter Rensky, on the other hand, linked his Orthodoxy closely to his Carpatho-Russian heritage and his concern for traditional values. Mariame Javic approached the faith on a more subjective and mystical level. These young adults sought to follow the whole Orthodox tradition yet their visions of the church remain different.

Such differing visions of Orthodoxy often included an eclectic approach in several of the subjects' adoption of the faith. Javic sees close similarities between the mysticism found in Buddhism and her Orthodox spirituality. Like many of the other subjects, she connected psychological health to her practice of Orthodox spirituality and viewed the sacramental nature of the church as enhancing her concern with the environment. While it is true that Orthodoxy teaches that spiritual perfection should affect all the components of a person, several of the subjects' emphasis on the connection of spirituality and emotional well-being sounded more contemporary than traditional. Wendy Kent valued the "wholistic" and "organic" qualities of Orthodoxy. Kent was involved in 12-step self-help programs before adopting Orthodoxy and she came naturally to the view that spirituality and the liturgy are "healthy" in much the same way that a New Age practitioner might cite the psychotherapeutic benefits of meditation. Gaglias, in contrast, was influenced by the new wave of evangelical leaders who have turned to Orthodoxy. His emphasis on defending the intellectual truth of Orthodoxy against other faiths shows some similarity to the conservative evangelical apologists who use biblical and historical "evidence" and rational arguments to win converts. In Gaglias' account, there was little emphasis on mystery and the non-rational component of Orthodoxy. Just why this pluralism and eclecticism was more pronounced among Orthodox subjects than the young traditionalists in the Catholic and Reformed traditions will be explored at the conclusion of this chapter.

Not Knowing Where God Isn't

The diversity among the Orthodox young adults in their faith often translated into an acceptance of pluralism in their relations outside of the church. Many of the subjects said that they had more non-Orthodox than Orthodox friends. Susan Miller said that the friends she has from the church exist in one orbit while friends from college days or work exist in another, "like two hermetically sealed worlds." She added that she spends "a lot more time in church just because it's an easy habit," rather than forming new social ties. Koulis said that she has more non-Orthodox than Orthodox friends, mainly because "I like people in general...I don't disregard people because they're not Orthodox. Who's to say that the Orthodox are the only ones to be saved?" She added, however, that she "witnesses" to her non-Christian friends, although usually only if they bring up spiritual matters first. Baumann said his involvement in the church is helping him to form more solid friendships with non-Orthodox friends. He said he is more capable of friendship since becoming Orthodox and now holds friends to a higher standard; Javic expressed similar sentiments on how her church friendships serve as a model for more secular relationships.

While Robin Genovese expressed concern over her conflict with the church about marrying a non-Orthodox man, she herself did not see such an action as wrong or sinful. Even now, Genovese said she does not pray that "God will make" her fiancée Orthodox. "I pray that we will love each other and be committed to each other. If that means him becoming Orthodox, great. If not, then that's the way we have to go." In her nine years of being in the Orthodox church, Genovese said that she had never dated Orthodox men. After her marriage she plans to bring any children she has to church (although they will not be baptized), but she is also considering sending them to Hebrew school. "That would be a good foundation for them. You really can't go wrong with that because Christianity came from Judaism," she said.

A similar degree of tolerance of religious differences emerged among most of the subjects in their personal relations. There was no one view among single subjects about whether they would marry only Orthodox partners. The men appeared to want only Orthodox partners more than the female subjects. While several said they had spoken to their friends about Orthodoxy, it was usually after someone had first expressed interest in the topic, and not always strictly for evangelistic reasons. Genovese said that "No one ever gets argued into the faith. I'll speak about my faith more because I want people to accept me and what I believe."

Mariame Javic said she makes no attempt to evangelize friends, believing that "God will lead them" to the faith if he chooses. "I don't want to take the responsibility for advising them. I don't have the power to do that. That's God's power." She added that "just because many of my friends don't go to church doesn't mean that they're not religious...The seeds of truth are spread everywhere. I respect a lot of people who are Catholic and people of other faiths. I just think my church is more beautiful for me." Javic's tolerance even extends to a prospective husband. "I would not even impose [my Orthodoxy] on him. But I would like an Orthodox wedding."

The more conservative Peter Rensky said that it is not necessary for a person to become Eastern Orthodox to find favor with God. "As long as you worship well and show reverence to God, you'll be accepted," he said. He added that since becoming Orthodox he has particularly come to respect Orthodox Jews and their devout lifestyle. Yet he does not like the fact that non-Christian and non-European-oriented groups are changing the cultural values of the country. He is troubled by the presence of Muslims in the U.S. "I will not patronize Muslim stores with my money. I'm not putting money into the hands of people hell-bent on killing us. They're one of the most hated enemies of Orthodoxy."

Intermingled with statements of religious tolerance were the subjects' frequent affirmations of the truth of Orthodoxy over other Christian denominations and the importance of adhering to a comprehensive tradition rather than to selective parts of the faith. Javic said that "If you belong to a religion you should believe all of it; you should take it seriously and try to understand it." She agreed with church teachings that Orthodoxy is the true church founded by Christ. When I asked her what she thought about the ecumenical movement's goal of church unity, she said the "church is [already] one. The church is the body of Christ, and Jesus is one; you can't slice him up." Baumann said that since becoming Orthodox he has felt more in common with traditional believers from other religions, such as Orthodox Jews, Muslims and Christians. He is also less interested than he used to be about efforts toward church unity with other Christians, particularly Protestants. "We have to envision unity with Rome. Catholic also have to realize that the action is in the East. It pains me to see the Roman Catholics fawning over Protestants as if they have anything to offer of real value." Rogoff said that "Orthodoxy is 100 percent pure, everything else is below 80 percent." Genovese added that

> Orthodoxy comes closest to the truth but I don't think we have it all. There's so much [convergence] in all the religions that I'm convinced that when we get to the next world, there's going to be Hindus, Muslims and Christians standing around saying to each other, 'Ah ha! So that's what that meant.'

Wendy Kent summed up the seemingly contradictory views of most subjects on the value of other churches and religions when she quoted the traditional Orthodox dictum, "We know where God is, but we don't know where he isn't."

An Orthodox Minority

While the Orthodox young adults tended to accept those with other beliefs, they often felt they were not tolerated in return. At one point in my interview with Robin Genovese at a coffee shop near her university, I noticed that she was speaking in hushed tones. As if to explain her change of voice, Genovese noted that she had just spotted a fellow teaching assistant who would not appreciate hearing comments about her spiritual life.

> The academy is extremely hostile to Christians...You're not considered intellectually viable if you're Christian. I don't even wear a cross. I wouldn't say grace in public if I were out with friends from school. It's a kind of bigotry that keeps me from doing what I want to do. I just wish people accepted other people more. I wish friends would be interested without sitting in judgment.

Susan Miller said she usually does not bring up her faith or religious concerns unless someone else does.

> I usually put challenges [to the faith] aside and say, 'Let's not get into this.' I would have to start from the beginning...You're making a statement about something you take seriously, but a lot of people today don't take it seriously. So people think it says something about you.

While subjects such as Baumann and Javic did not necessarily feel any conflict with society because of their beliefs, most of the Orthodox young adults believed they were a minority in a hostile and indifferent society. Gaglias wears a huge cross around his neck and said he speaks openly of his faith while at work at the diner. But he said that he is more often met with indifference rather than curiosity and interest. He added that he is angry that Christianity seems to be increasingly discriminated against. "In public agencies you're not allowed to wear a cross, but you can wear skull cap or anything else having to do with another religion," he said. Jill Cook said misunderstanding and non-acceptance is a normal part of being Christian, particularly being Orthodox. "Try not eating for a few days, and see what people think. Part of being in the church is that the world is not going to understand."

Between Two Worlds

The move to Eastern Orthodoxy did not generate drastic changes in most of the young adults' lifestyles. There was a very gradual change in sexual attitudes and practices among several of the subjects after they moved to the Orthodox church. John Gaglias said that he remained in sexual relations with women after returning to the church, but over time changed his dating lifestyle, enjoying longer-term relations that focused on friendship and a common faith rather than sexuality. Several of the subjects practiced premarital sex within relationships before they returned to or adopted the faith and they retained relatively liberal attitudes on sexuality afterwards. Genovese said, "I was very different in my starting point than other people in relation to celibacy. I was sexually active early in life and was not raised valuing chastity." After her conversion she continued to have sexual relations, although they were rarely casual. "On one hand, I felt what I was doing was right, but I also agreed with the church's teachings, so there was this tension. Sometimes the church sounded like this external voice that didn't take into account where I was." More recently, Genovese has "felt uncomfortable" with the level of sexual involvement she had had with her fiancée and the tensions this has caused her in relation to the church and has sought to live more within church guidelines.

Mariame Javic was involved in a serious relationship with a man that was leading to marriage when she first came to Orthodoxy. With her priest's guidance she did not partake of communion while she was involved in sexual relations. Javic, whose relationship ended short of marriage, said that she still thinks premarital sexual involvement is permissible if the couple is committed to each other and are considering marriage; "You have to know who you are marrying," she added. She agrees with a priest who told her, "the faster you get married the faster you get divorced." In listening to the subjects, it wasn't difficult to get the impression that some had a double standard on sexuality: they were sexually active at certain periods of their lives while at the same time practicing a faith that called such activity a sin. Susan Miller, who also had relationships including sexual involvement while being in the faith, said the relatively lax approach she and others follow on sexuality is in keeping with the "tendency of Orthodoxy to be flexible, to set up the ideal and then to recognize that you can't always live up to it. You realize you didn't [live up to the ideal on sexual faithfulness] and say, well, I've made a mistake."

If sexuality posed some unresolved tensions for the Orthodox young adults, the appreciation of popular culture presented fewer dilemmas. Most of the subjects said they have not changed their tastes in popular music and other forms of entertainment since they moved to the faith. There were some exceptions. Rogoff said that he no longer watches television because of the lack of "uplifting programs," and today mainly reads books on the lives of the saints rather than secular books. Only Rogoff and Gaglias sharply restricted their viewing and listening habits because of their Orthodox faith, which meant limiting R-rated movies and listening to far less popular music, such as rock. Other young adults reported only small changes in consumption of popular culture. Baumann said that he is more sensitive about profanity being used in such media since becoming Orthodox. Genovese said she had no problem viewing R-rated films, adding that "If they're a little racy it doesn't bother me." Mariame Javic's appreciation of experimental, avant-garde film and art and a wide variety of music, such as rap, rock and reggae, has not changed with her move to Orthodoxy. Most of the young adults did report they now also frequently listen to Orthodox church music. When the controversy was raging a few years ago about federal funding for the sexually explicit artwork of David Mapplethorpe and other artists, Javic took the side of the criticized artists and against what she saw as attempts at censorship. She even defended her position at a church meeting and was glad to find that her priest agreed with her.

A greater tension between traditional and modern worldviews came out clearly on the topic of gender roles and feminism. After she converted to Orthodoxy as a teenager, Miller said she went through an "anti-feminist" period, but added that "a few years in the working world cured me of that." She opposes radical feminist ideas viewing men as the oppressors of women because "they tend to dehumanize people as some kind of artificial entities." On husband-wife relations, she said that the husband will not always be the leader, since "situations vary from family to family." She said that women are discriminated against both in the workplace and in church. "It's hard as a women to be active in church doing anything but baking cookies." But she views such exclusion in the church having as much to do with clericalism as inequality. The Orthodox priest is often delegated duties that lay people can perform. Although she said that "on theological grounds the jury is out" about women's ordination, pressing for such a change would only add to current divisions among the Orthodox.

Robin Genovese said that she is "unabashedly for women's rights" and believes that

> women could do almost anything as well as or better than men. But I also definitely believe in gender roles. I don't want to have that thrust aside. I love the idea of being a wife. I have no problem with the husband being the head of the family. Saint Paul taught that husbands are the head of a wife. But I wouldn't put up with a husband who would not see me as an equal. I would only subordinate myself to someone who would not consider me inferior.

While she supports the church's rule of ordaining only men as priests, Genovese added, "I don't know why there are no women in the diaconate or tonsored to be [scripture] readers." Jill Cook was more critical of the prohibition against women priests. "I don't pretend to know more than 2,000 years of tradition, but I've never heard an argument that has convinced me that [the ordination of women as priests] is wrong." She added, however, that the women's ordination issue is "so bound up with talk of rights. It goes with a pride that 'we know better, that we're victims and oppressed.' You hardly ever hear feminists talk of sin." Aside from her qualified support for women's ordination, Cook had conservative views on the family; she held to the view that the husband should be the head of a family. Interestingly, fellow former Episcopalian Wendy Kent said she was "strongly opposed" to women priests, yet she was more willing than Cook to interpret the biblical teachings on marriage to mean that women and men are equal in authority in the relationship. She also was critical of the writings of some early church fathers and saints about their negative attitudes toward women. "The way some of the church fathers speak of women, they don't really seem knowledgeable about women. There does seem to be a strand of thought in the church writings [on women] that doesn't seem right."

Mariame Javic said that feminism "damaged women a lot, although it also did some good. It made women more confident." She is particularly troubled by the view in some feminist circles that women are powerless and that there are few differences between the sexes. She said that

> Women have power as much as men, but its a different kind of power. For instance, the father usually lays down the law in families. A wise women will not fight the man, but wait for a time to suggest something different. Part of a women's nature is different than the nature of men. Women can accept humility, while men have a lot more pride to overcome to be spiritual...I don't think the church is biased against women. We have the Theotokos [Mary] and so many strong women as examples.

She did agree with the other women subjects in holding that the diaconate should be open to women. Javic added, "it would be a privilege to be a mother because I would be imitating the Mother of God." But she did not want to limit women only to motherhood or homemaking. "Women should do what they want. I have no problem with a man staying at home and the woman working. Not all men are the same. It's hard to generalize because we're all different. We all have characteristics of the other [sex] in us. Anthropology teaches that." The male subjects had similar conflicting feelings about gender roles and feminism. Baumann said that while women in general should take a greater role in childrearing than men, he could see many exceptions to this rule. "With my hours as a teacher I'll probably be more involved in child raising." He said he does not believe marriages should be based on equality, but rather on the husband and wife complimenting each other. "Each couple is unique. There will be more aggressive women who take more of a leadership role in the marriage. I have no problems with that." Even Peter Rensky, who was more conservative on most issues than the other respondents, said that he bases his marriage more on equality between partners than "headship" of the husband over the wife.

The issue of gay rights and homosexuality also elicited views that are difficult to categorize in the usual "liberal versus conservative" framework. While no subjects defended homosexual relations or gave much support to the gay rights movement, they often stated that they did not wish to judge homosexuals or make a political issue of their beliefs. Mariame Javic said,

> Who am I to judge others? It's not the most important sin. There
> are sins like gluttony that no one talks about. I don't go to church
> to hear that you shouldn't be homosexual. I go to church to hear
> that if I go on sinning my soul will die. People are using [the
> emphasis on homosexuality as sin] as a political issue.

She was equally against the gay rights movement pressing for
special legislation to protect homosexuals. "I have friends who are gay,
but I don't think of them as my gay friends, just as my friends.
Everything is being used in a political way today. I don't understand
why Americans make a political movement out of what they do in
their bedrooms." Wendy Kent expressed similar sentiments, asking,
"Why legislation? I don't understand why we need legislation to treat
human beings as human beings." She added, however, that "if such
legislation is necessary [to insure against discrimination], I would not
oppose it." Baumann said that while he does not want discrimination
against gays, he said he is "extremely opposed to gay rights
legislation," because it "exploits the civil rights of blacks." The
attempt to link discrimination against homosexuals to the
discrimination suffered by blacks is "racist" and downplays the real
differences between race and sexual feelings and behavior, he added.
Genovese added that she has "mixed feelings" on the issue of
homosexuality. Both my fiancée and I have friends who are gay. It's
not something easy for them. It's not like putting on and off a suit. I
really can't judge them."

Turning From The Political To The Personal

In interviewing Orthodox subjects, I soon discovered the questions
I had asked the Catholic and Calvinist young traditionalists did not
always resonate well with these young adults—especially when they
touched on politics. As I delved deeper into such matters as health
care, abortion and the economy with Mariame Javic, she shook her
head more than once, prefacing her often knowledgeable remarks with
the rejoinder, "More politics. Look, I am not very political, but..." Jeff
Rogoff would often cut off my questions with the protest, "That's a
worldly matter. I have no opinion." Javic's and Rogoff's disregard for
political matters was not uncommon among the subjects. Most of the
young adults agreed that since becoming Orthodox they are less active

or no more active and concerned on political issues than previously. Such inactivity included not voting in national and local elections, paying less attention to current political issues, and less involvement in social activism. Rogoff said that since his return to Orthodoxy, his "cause is in getting my own life together...We should pray for leaders. I don't want society to become barbarian, but I think it's better for the Christian to be quiet and pray. Prayer is the strongest weapon."

Javic echoed such views, saying that she is "trying to change things in my little part of the world. Politics is a corrupt and dirty game." Robin Genovese said that since becoming Orthodox she is "much more cynical about the good we can do politically. We're better off acting on an individual level or on a subversive level, which would challenge certain structures and policies. I think political groups have a dangerous tendency to think things are perfectible." Jill Cook was involved in the peace movement before becoming Orthodox, but today she said she tends to "live on a more local, personal level. If I'm going to be against abortion, it's probably not going to be marching. Instead, I'd adopt a baby. I'm not as likely to go out and protest for peace as I did in the past; now I'd treat people nicer on the cafeteria line." Cook said that her move away from larger political action toward the personal arena may be due to the "sense of personal responsibility" she has gained in her Orthodox prayer life as well as because of the "focus on the person [rather than abstractions and generalities] found in Orthodox theology."

Only Peter Rensky said that his move to Orthodoxy was part of the transition to a more politically activist and conservative stance, such as on pro-life issues and preserving traditional values. While John Gaglias said he is more likely to take voting seriously since returning to the faith, he also noted that he is less concerned with current events. He no longer reads the newspaper—"except the sports page"— believing that "the most important news and signs of the times are found in the Bible, like the book of Revelations...I also feel like I'm protecting my soul [in not reading the newspaper]" from distractions and unspiritual influences.

Church involvement in political issues was even more strongly opposed by almost all the subjects. Baumann said that such opposition stemmed from Orthodox teachings. "The primary service of the church to the world is its liturgical life. Most of the other things the church does, such as its social services, can be done better by the world." The idea of greater Orthodox influence in society through political means was often dismissed as unrealistic or even utopian. Miller added that all attempts "to establish a Christian society have failed miserably— they ended up discrediting the church and making it less loving toward others. If every one was the same some think we would have our problems solved, but we wouldn't." Javic viewed the bloodshed in the former Yugoslavia with scorn. "I don't like it when people use Orthodoxy for politics. [Orthodoxy] is only a spiritual life. I don't think [those engaged in warfare] are really being religious in Serbia." Only Rensky, with his strong emphasis on traditional values and ethnic Orthodoxy, wanted to reinstill Christian values in public and said, "We shouldn't start changing U.S. laws and the constitution which were based on Christianity." He added, however, that one should not be a "fanatic," and that it would be impractical to enforce Christian laws, such as blue laws and a law against adultery.

The intensity of many subjects' disdain for Orthodox political involvement was expressed in their views on abortion. Only in recent years have the various Orthodox churches become involved in pro-life issues. Although not as involved politically in pro-life issues as the Roman Catholics and evangelicals, there is a growing segment of Orthodox believers involved in anti-abortion activism. Javic said that when a bishop started speaking on pro-life issues during one service, she and some of her friends walked out of the church in protest. "There we were all spiritual and boom—abortion! The church is no place to teach politics. The church shouldn't worry about being contemporary. It's timeless." Robin Genovese said,

> I'm unbelievably angry that abortion has become such a political issue. It's a personal issue. I don't believe in abortion, but it doesn't do any good to force people to accept my views. I refuse to participate in the debate either on the pro-choice or pro-life side. Both sides are more interested in politics than spirituality.

Miller voiced similar concerns.

> I don't think the pro-life political movement belongs in the church. I find the people who are involved in [the pro-life movement] deeply offensive to the same religion which claims that the act [of abortion] is inhumane. The relationship between mother and child is unique and it shouldn't be made into a political issue—it dehumanizes both the mother and the child.

Even though Baumann is strongly against the act of abortion, he said "it's a problem of consumerist and corporate interest. Making it illegal would not solve these problems. It's all about the myth of the American dream that no one is free until they're free of everyone else." Wendy Kent said she is more likely to take part in pro-life activities, such as marches and protests, since becoming Orthodox, although she has not yet done so. "I don't think we hold human life very high. We're becoming a society of self-centered people and I don't think that's going to lead anywhere." She added, however, that abortion is a "messy issue. People are not telling the truth about every thing on both sides" of the conflict. Subjects in favor of changing the abortion laws in the U.S., such as Peter Rensky, Eileen Koulis, and John Gaglias, were undecided about whether they would take part in pro-life activism.

The rejection of political activism among most of the subjects did not necessarily mean that they were unconcerned with social and political issues. For instance, several of the subjects showed strong support for environmental concern, even to the extent of calling for church support of such issues. Susan Miller said that environmental issues "are very important and don't get the attention they should in the church. The church should speak out [on environmentalism] because it's a question of the stewardship of the planet." Javic said that her concern about environmental issues, including the prevention of cruelty to animals, is the "only way I have been political." She added, however, that recycling and other activities should be run by community-based efforts rather than by the government. Genovese said that while Christians should be concerned about stewardship of the environment, they should not be influenced by "fascist" environmental groups that have utopian ideologies.

There was a strong pacifist, non-interventionist sentiment among several subjects. Rogoff said that since returning to the church he has embraced a stance of nonviolence, which would include being a conscientious objector. He said that "Being in the world is very disturbing, but the Christian does not fight with the sword but with peace and meekness. That's a kind of power. It's not passivity." Gaglias turned down a high paying position working in an engineering plant because the firm had a contract with a weapons company. Javic has become strongly pacifist since becoming Orthodox, saying she would not resist or respond violently to being attacked on New York streets. But, as with the other subjects, she was not prescribing pacifism as a political policy for governments but rather as a matter of personal commitment that has to be taken up voluntarily.

Only Wendy Kent and Jill Cook edged toward taking a more political pacifist stance. Kent said that if the U.S. started bombing Serbia or Bosnia she would probably become active in opposing such intervention. Since becoming Orthodox, she has come to "hate the way the war is portrayed in the media." Kent added, "It's a bad scene, but no one is guilt-free. The [Serbian Orthodox leader] Patriarch Paul has said it best: 'stop the killing'". But the move to Orthodoxy did not always lead to pacifism. Baumann said he has come to a greater appreciation of the historic Christian teaching on "just wars," holding that armed conflict may be necessary and can serve a moral cause. On the issue of pacifism, Miller said it would be "naive to remove yourself from all armed conflict." Rensky said that he "has a lot of affinity" for the Serbians because of their similar Eastern European, Orthodox background. He also agrees with the Serbian concern about the "ascendancy of a [Bosnian] Muslim state in Europe." He said that the U.S. should not bomb the Serbs, but added that the Bosnian Muslims should have been allowed weapons earlier on in the conflict so they could have defended themselves in the ensuing conflict with the Serbians.

On other political issues, the subjects ranged from conservative to moderate to liberal. All of the subjects were opposed to the death penalty (although most Orthodox churches do not have official positions on the death penalty), except for Gaglias, who was undecided, and Rensky, who was a strong supporter of such a measure. On questions of the economy and how best to help the poor, there was a division between those calling for continued state assistance and those more suspicious of state control. Baumann said that he has "no problem with the West European social democracies with mixed economies. Sometimes I wish I'd been born in Canada. America is definitely the odd man out." When asked about the best way to help the poor, Baumann answered without hesitation, "Tax the corporations, tax the rich." Javic said that socialism is more compatable with Christianity on principle since it is based on sharing and cooperation rather than competition, although she was against a centralized economy and government. Genovese said that the best way to help people is "one-on-one," something she is working on through her teaching disadvantaged students. Miller sees a "reformed capitalism," as the best hope for America and repudiates socialism, especially after having seen this economic system at work in Eastern Europe. Rensky was the furthest to the right, saying the "smaller the government the better," and that welfare should be "almost cut entirely."

Transcending The Culture Wars

The young adults' accounts of how their faith affects their social views were as diverse as their journeys into Orthodoxy. Mariame Javic saw her Orthodox faith as promoting tolerance toward others, non-violence and identification with the poor; she said Orthodoxy moved her in the direction of living more simply. Peter Rensky reported few changes in his way of living and stressed the importance of group solidarity and traditional values in his faith. He was not hesitant in stating that Muslims have been and still are the enemies of his faith. Susan Miller was a centrist in her social and political views and was concerned that Orthodoxy help its members integrate church teachings with their lives in a way that would not reject the modern world and its problems. A major example of the political differences between the subjects emerged over the pro-life movement. Several of the subjects cited the role of their faith as making them more wary of such a cause, while others said their faith made them more supportive of the pro-life movement, though not necessarily more involved pro-life activism. Such divergences are not simply a matter of these young adults belonging to different parishes with different teachings. It was not uncommon to find members of the same parish, such as Baumann, Miller, and Javic, who had different perspectives on many issues.

The young adults came to Orthodoxy with diverse lifestyles and outlooks on life and most appeared to have retained these values years after having embraced the faith. Robin Genovese spoke for most of the subjects when she said, "The church serves more as a reminder of what my values have always been." In Genovese's case such instilled values were tolerance and kindness toward others rather than a strict code of sexual morality and social activism. In her four years of intense Orthodox devotion, Javic has retained her pre-Orthodox love for popular music forms and experimental art. Her negative view of politics appear to stem more from her Eastern European background than from teachings she has received in the Orthodox church.

What is the reason for the subjects' relatively high degree of pluralism in their social outlook and their general acceptance of secular culture? Part of the answer can be found in the Eastern Orthodox tradition itself. As Susan Miller said in discussing sexuality, there is the "tendency of Orthodoxy to be flexible, to set up the ideal and then to recognize that you can't always live up to it." The social space in Orthodoxy that exists between the church's ideals and its tolerance of members who are "working out their salvation," permits a greater diversity of attitudes and behavior than found in more tightly knit and stricter religious groups. In a similar way, the Orthodox belief that God works outside one's own community—a tenet emphasized by all the subjects to one degree or another—seems to have encouraged a good deal of tolerance and acceptance of pluralism among these young adults. Orthodoxy is also highly decentralized and does not have an authoritative teaching office or magisterium that might encourage more uniformity of views.

The Orthodox liturgy, the central and sometimes only function of many parishes, also illustrates and may even help explain the "loose-fitting," flexible nature of the faith. Parishioners come late and leave early, with many not staying for the entire service. During the chanting and corporate prayers, parishioners can be seen crossing themselves at different times and moving around the sanctuary as they light candles and venerate and pray before various icons. The sense of individual freedom allowed in the liturgy appears to have been carried over by the subjects into other parts of their lives. Robin Genovese exhibited this kind of individualism in her account of discovering Orthodoxy when she said she felt she didn't have her "individuality threatened by social standards" as in other congregations. It is not difficult to see a certain fit between the individuality and diversity accepted within Orthodoxy and the modern condition of individualism and pluralism.

It is evident that the subjects' Orthodox faith did not locate them within a community of like-minded believers who shared common social and cultural views. These young adults were not necessarily looking for such an intimate community in the first place. Rather, they were searching for a faith that offered them an ideal vision of spiritual truth (through the liturgy and church traditions and teachings) and the tools (through the spiritual disciplines) by which they could find such a reality in their own lives. The themes of pluralism and individualism, however, do not tell the whole story about the young adult movement to Orthodoxy. All of the subjects, including the ethnic-oriented Peter Rensky, cited the importance of the liturgy and spiritual disciplines in their lives, even if their observance of such practices was irregular. All of the subjects had close connections with their parishes. They all said they have benefited from the guidance they find in their relationship with priests and spiritual confessors. It is these central spiritual components of the faith rather than that of a common worldview which provides the bond between these young adults.

In one of the few scholarly studies of American Orthodox converts, researchers H.B. Cavalcanti and H. Paul Chalfont found a unique sense of community among the Orthodox. The researchers interviewed 25 Orthodox converts in Boston—who were mostly young adults—and found that they were drawn to the church through "the liturgy, the seasons of fasting, [and] the collective life of the community of faith." Cavalcanti and Chalfont found the converts

> not simply robotic followers of a rigid faith. Rather, they bounce their individual, implicit feelings off the traditions of the Orthodox faith. It is not that they abandon individual feelings but that what are still their individual understandings or private belief systems find communal support, despite differential interpretations, in the collective life that gives validation to their own social construction of reality.[18]

In other words, the common liturgy and spiritual disciplines still preserved within Orthodoxy provides believers with such a collective life while also allowing a good deal of freedom in social outlook and lifestyle.

While the adoption and return to Orthodoxy did not have a strong impact on many aspects of the young adults' lifestyles and social outlooks, this does not mean they were or are unchanged by their faith. Jill Cook's relationship with her father confessor helped change her negative attitudes toward men and turned her toward considering marriage; Mariame Javic said she hated "weak" people before becoming Orthodox but now feels a special affection for them. John Gaglias changed his relations with women from seeking sexual gratification to long-term friendships with them. The practice of spiritual disciplines were claimed to be often directly related to such changes. Nevertheless, it is true that these changes were more likely to remain on personal and inter-personal levels rather than finding expression on a larger social scale.

One hears in the subjects' accounts a turning inward toward spiritual matters and a shift away from public concern. To put it simply, there were few calls to revive an Orthodox culture modeled after Byzantium. This tendency may again be related to the dynamics of Orthodoxy. The liturgy and the church itself is viewed as the manifestation of the kingdom of God on earth. While there is also the Orthodox teaching that the world is being transformed into the kingdom of God, the church is still seen as the focal point of God's "action" in the world. The dominant (though not the only) form of spirituality in Orthodoxy has been shaped by its monastic tradition emphasizing an ascetic life based on contemplation and prayer and removed from the concerns of the world. That such a tendency is not uncommon among the Orthodox could be seen in even such a conservative pro-life activist and cultural warrior as Frank Schaeffer, who has come to the position that the most important task of Orthodoxy in America is to revive its monastic tradition. In Schaeffer's recent writings and lectures, he is much more outspoken in criticizing materialism and the success-driven "American way of life" than he was in his evangelical Protestant days.[19]

Several of the subjects showed signs of at least a semi-monastic lifestyle. Simeon Baumann and Mariame Javic often use their chrismated names to emphasize their Orthodox identity, just as a monk would take on a new name upon joining a monastery; Javic now lives a more simple lifestyle; John Gaglias has stopped reading the newspaper to protect the state of his spiritual life; Michael Rogoff avoids the "worldly" entanglements of television and popular music. It should be remembered that there was also a concern among a minority of the subjects, such as Susan Miller, that Orthodoxy needs to have a more positive relationship to modern society and help its members relate its spirituality and teachings to secular life and work.

It is no coincidence that the subjects most involved in such ascetic-based spiritual disciplines were also the least politically active and concerned. The spiritual life was often seen to be in conflict with political and worldly concerns—whether this took place in the wider society or within the church. I often wondered why there was more opposition among several subjects to church involvement in the anti-abortion movement than to church involvement in environmentalism or other causes. For such subjects the pro-life movement was seen as the most politically explosive issue today. Thus, bringing this movement into the church would serve to politicize Orthodoxy and dilute it of its spiritual and transcendental content. Of course, pro-life concern in the church can be (and has been by Orthodox church leaders, laity, as well as by the other subjects) interpreted in a more positive vein (i.e., that the church is helping to safeguard the sacredness of life), but for a segment of subjects, the issue serves as a distraction from the spiritual nature and mission of the church.

The difficulty in categorizing the subjects' political beliefs is another sign of their avoidance of a commitment to political ideology. Most eschewed "conservative" and "liberal" labels and were not hesitant to borrow views from either camp, as in the case of Simeon Baumann supporting a larger welfare state while opposing abortion on demand and the gay rights movement. In a similar manner, most subjects lamented the "politics" that take place within Orthodox bodies and jurisdictions and the divisions that result from them. Even the minority of subjects who saw the possibility of ordaining women to the priesthood backed away from enlisting in such a cause because of this issue's strongly political and divisive nature and its association in some cases with the feminist concern for power and equal rights within mainline Protestant denominations. What is evident in the subjects' accounts is their concern for the primacy of the spiritual and the personal over politics and ideology. The subjects' concern for the personal over political and ideological causes was expressed in the common refrain, "I can't judge them," when speaking about groups or individuals involved in a wide range of activities—from sexual activity to accruing wealth. In fact, being non-judgmental about people was often cited as an important spiritual virtue by these young adults.

The almost unanimous condemnation of capital punishment (although most Orthodox bodies have not made statements on this issue) and the fair number of subjects who have moved toward greater acceptance of nonviolence as a lifestyle (although not as part of a political agenda) may also show the subjects' focus on the importance of the individual over the political and ideological. Such a pacifist tendency may not be unique to the subjects; Orthodox writer

Alexander Webster has noted that pacifism is currently finding a greater hearing in Orthodox circles.[20]

Many of the issues that have been politicized by protagonists on both sides of the "culture wars," such as concerning feminism, gay rights, and the role of the state in meeting human needs, were viewed in a different light by most of these Orthodox young adults. Most of them could be called moderate feminists; they favored opening the office of the diaconate (though not the priesthood) to women—a position viewed as liberal by more traditional Orthodox believers. On the issue of sex roles there was the common view among most subjects that one should not fit the sexes into stereotypical roles, such as that the husband must be the sole leader and provider for the family. In the same way, some varieties of feminism were often criticized for seeking to level the differences between the sexes and stigmatize men as oppressors and women as victims, again revealing the Orthodox concern with the personal over the ideological dimension of life. This alternative way of looking at the gender issue was reflected in the comment by Mariame Javic that "It's hard to generalize [about sex roles] because we're all different. We all have characteristics of the other sex in us..." Such a view is not necessarily in conflict with Eastern Orthodoxy. Orthodox spirituality has taught that the soul has feminine and masculine components.

In their research on Orthodox converts, Cavalcanti and Chalfont found that the faith appealed to these young adults as it offered them a "unique opportunity for contending with modernity because theology in the Eastern tradition differs markedly from that in the West— whether Roman Catholicism or Protestantism." In contrast to Western thought where all truth is viewed in an "either-or-matter," the researchers maintain that Eastern thought holds that "one can believe on different levels and that beliefs held on one level need not be consistent with those on another." Thus, conflicts between science and faith—or between modern gender relations and the teachings of the church fathers—can be "avoided simply because when one thinks theologically it is on one level; scientific thought is on another level."[21]

Of course, the views of Orthodox converts, particularly the clergy and other leaders, can be very conservative; in reading their literature one can find vigorous condemnations of feminism, theological liberalism, individualism, ecumenism, and many other modern currents.[22] The recent wave of converts to Orthodoxy from evangelical Protestantism has created a more dogmatic and polemical strain in the American church—a fact that increasingly concerns some Orthodox leaders and intellectuals. For instance, Orthodox theologian Vigen Guroian charges that such an influential convert as Frank Schaeffer is bringing an alien "fundamentalist" mind-set into Orthodoxy through his literalistic reading of "Holy Tradition," and his view that Orthodoxy represents a "remedy for cultural crisis and moral malaise." Guroian argues that such a reading of the faith eclipses the Orthodox emphasis on mystery and the ecumenical nature of the church.[23]

The new evangelical influence in Orthodoxy was evident in several of the subjects' accounts, especially in Greek Orthodox John Gaglias' adamant attempts to prove the "truth" of his faith to unbelievers. But the mystical and decentralized nature of Orthodoxy can also lead to a more adaptive and flexible posture in relation to modernity. For most of the subjects, Orthodoxy represents a transcendent alternative and, in some cases, an escape from the culture wars and the increasing politicization of society. It remains to be seen whether Orthodoxy itself can remain free from such influences, and whether believers can escape from such political and social conflicts without becoming irrelevant to the society in which they are called to live out their faith.

CHAPTER 4:

Comparisons and Conclusions

As I was nearing the completion of my interviews, I sometimes wondered what would happen if all the subjects were gathered together in one room. What would Bill Wenzel with his rigorous, all-embracing Calvinism have to say to Mariame Javic and her mystical and tolerant Orthodoxy or to James Ryan with his highly private yet deeply felt traditional Catholic faith? Of course, many of the other subjects, especially the Reformed and conservative Catholics, had a good deal in common. But, on first impression at least, it is the differences rather than the commonalities among the young traditionalists that stand out and demand attention. It was becoming obvious that I was not so much dealing with a turn to "tradition" as much as a turn to "traditions" with very different histories, theologies, spiritualities, and ways of relating to the world. Within such traditions, many of the young adults have located themselves in groups that have sought to recapture the purity of these faiths.

Community And Countercultures

A comparison of the three traditions for the degree of community they have generated among the young adults provides an interesting twist on the maxim that Catholicism and Orthodoxy are communal religions while Protestantism, especially Calvinism, is an individualistic one. Both the Reformed and the Orthodox subjects found a faith which gave them a strong sense of community, yet the two faiths offered contrasting models of community life. The conservative Reformed congregations served as a social as well as a spiritual center that directed the young adults toward a unified and comprehensive "Christian worldview" that could be practically applied to everyday life. As a result, the Reformed faith had dramatic implications for the subjects' social and political lives. The conservative Reformed form of community was reinforced by a network of united families which perform similar educational and communal functions to that of the congregation.

The Eastern Orthodox parishes and priests created a community based on common rituals (the liturgy and spiritual disciplines) and mentoring structures which imparted to the young adults a strong spiritual bond and identity. The Orthodox, however, also allowed for a larger degree of pluralism and individualism among its members in their lifestyles and social views than found among the other groups.

While some of the Catholic subjects found a sense of community in the new conservative religious orders and Latin Masses (though quite different from the older Catholic conceptions of community often based on birth, ethnicity and neighborhood), they were looking more for a sense of tradition and authority in their personal lives. Several of the Catholic young adults appeared to remain as individualists even after they embraced traditional religiosity. This is especially the case with the traditionalist Catholics, who, in the words of writer Charles Coulombe, have to do "an awful lot of searching" to maintain their faith. The vast size of the Catholic Church and its impersonal liturgy (a trait the church shares with Eastern Orthodoxy) makes it easier to remain an individualist in that faith than in smaller bodies where believers are enmeshed in close bonds of fellowship and take a more active part in church services. Catholicism has been influenced to a greater degree by currents of secularization and pluralism than has Eastern Orthodoxy and the conservative Reformed churches, so it is not too surprising that the move toward traditional religiosity for these subjects was fraught with a good deal of conflict, individual effort, and even isolation. As noted in the chapter on Catholicism, the process of identifying what is "traditional" or "conservative" in the faith is precarious enough. What one Catholic may view as a return to tradition, such as a devotion to the Latin Mass and the practice of hierarchical marriage roles, may be seen by another Catholic as outdated and antithetical to "authentic" tradition.

The Catholics were the most troubled about their own religious body. They were critical of many aspects about their church—its leadership, schools, recent teachings, its ineffectiveness in secular society, and about fellow Catholics whom they felt were not serious about or loyal to the faith. The Calvinists and Orthodox were clearly appreciative of their denominations, although the latter were more likely to complain about the politics, ethnic divisions, and other shortcomings in their churches. The Catholics were also more likely to experience conflict with the older generations in their church (especially the older baby boomers) than the other subjects, often making the claim that they felt robbed of their heritage because of the changes made by older generations after Vatican II.

The tension between holding to a traditional faith and living in the modern society was felt by all the young traditionalists. While the hunger for community is an important motivation in becoming involved in traditional religion, it should be emphasized that the 30 young adults are all individualists and non-conformists in relation to American society; they have distinctive beliefs and lifestyles that are in sharp contrast to the high levels of conformity often found among younger generations. Many reported that their beliefs were often regarded as strange or irrelevant and that they felt like minorities in society. The Reformed subjects' attempt to follow their faith and formulate a "Christian worldview" appeared to have the greatest impact—and exacted the highest cost—on their social and family lives, educations, and careers (due to Sabbath observance, for instance). The Reformed young adults, whose theology of antithesis (that Christian and non-Christian worldviews are fundamentally incompatible) made them more accepting of their minority status, belong to a strong counterculture that provides its members with alternatives to secular society in social life and education. They are also more likely to be able to pass on the faith to their children.

The Catholic subjects, especially the members of the conservative Franciscan lay order, were similar to the Reformed believers in their changed lifestyles involving areas of entertainment and sexuality, as well as in their greater involvement in activism on pro-life and other family issues and support for conservative political causes. But while they and conservative Catholics in general speak of forming a counterculture, such a task may be difficult to carry out. Because of the pluralism in the church, the more individualistic Catholic subjects appear to have less of a support system to sustain such a counterculture; it makes it difficult for parents to pass down the faith when they mistrust the Catholic schools and are not themselves strongly rooted in parish life. The pluralism within the church has prompted conservative Catholics to in effect build a separate counterculture (through their own schools, press and other organizations) within American Catholicism.

The traditionalist-oriented subjects (i.e., those devoted to the Latin Mass) showed more acceptance of modern culture and lifestyles (ranging from greater sexual involvement to having more non-Catholic friends) than the conservative Catholics, while also supporting pro-life activism and conservative social and political views. The traditionalists' greater acceptance of modern culture and lifestyles is similar to that of the Eastern Orthodox subjects. It may be that the highly ritualistic and impersonal nature of both the Latin Mass and the Orthodox liturgy conveys a sense of the mystical and transcendent for these subjects, but is not easily translated into an internalized set of practical rules of behavior. In contrast with the other subjects, the Orthodox subjects also showed no greater (and, in many cases, less) political involvement and consensus on social and political issues due to their adoption of the faith. But it would be incorrect to say that Orthodoxy had little effect on the subjects' lives. The Orthodox young adults were more likely than those in the other groups to report that the practice of their faith resulted in greater psychological well-being and improved interpersonal relations, such as in feeling and expressing greater tolerance and compassion toward others.

A Conservative Ecumenism

For all their differences, it is evident that a kind of "conservative ecumenism" had developed among the young traditionalists, reflecting a new pattern of closer relations between the wider movements of conservative Catholics, Orthodox and evangelical Protestants on both social and religious issues. That such an alliance is particularly strong among young Christians is evident in the recent founding of the *Regeneration Quarterly*, a national journal started by conservative Protestant, Catholic and Orthodox young adults that seeks to explore the similarities and differences among these traditions and "recover the insights of the early church for our postmodern movement."[1] Many of the young adults interviewed expressed a desire for closer relations with other traditional or conservative Christians. Their adherence to orthodox Christian doctrines and opposition to liberal influences in their respective churches places these young adults in a loosely bound coalition that can be seen as ecumenical, although it is not exactly what the National and World Council of Churches would mean by the term. This was especially the case with the Catholic and Reformed subjects, whose common concern with abortion and other culture war issues made them strong allies in activism. That the alliance on social issues also touches on faith concerns is demonstrated in the accounts of Reformed subjects, whose tradition has historically been in strong opposition to Roman Catholicism. Most of the subjects said that their work on pro-life issues has served to convince them that Catholics can also be Christians. It is also true, however, that where there was less agreement on culture war issues, such as between the Reformed and several of the Eastern Orthodox young adults, there was also fewer bonds based on faith. This may mean that when the culture wars fade from significance, divisions based on theology and doctrine will be revived.

Regardless of whether they considered themselves more or less interested in politics and culture war issues, most of the young traditionalists expressed a disillusionment with the political process, particularly as it is expressed on the national level. Several of the Orthodox young adults often eschewed political participation as a distraction from spiritual concerns. Other Orthodox subjects and most of the Catholic and Reformed young adults did not hold high hopes for national political change and focused most of their attention on local and family-based issues. The Catholic and Reformed young adults' pessimism about large-scale political change may be related to their negative views of the Clinton administration and the damage they feel its policies are causing in the country. In this case, the change to a more conservative government that emerged after the 1994 elections might elicit greater optimism about national politics, although it is not yet clear that a more Republican congress will address abortion, gay rights, and other contentious issues to the satisfaction of the Reformed and Catholic subjects. In reading the literature published by the movements and churches to which these young traditionalists belong, one finds a greater degree of engagement and interest in larger political issues than expressed in this study (including the Eastern Orthodox). It may well be that the 30 young adults are not representative of their church bodies in their political views and involvement. Then again, such literature may reflect the "official" views of these groups' leaderships rather than those of their constituencies.

The young traditionalists' distrust of political institutions does seem to be related to developments taking place among the younger generations in general. In an overview of research on baby boomers, Paul C. Light writes that this generation has continuously showed little confidence in political institutions. Light adds that the upheavals of the 1960s, as well as Watergate and other subsequent crises, may have helped cause an estrangement from political institutions. He notes that baby boomers have not lost faith in the basic American system of government or the free enterprise system but rather in the ability of large institutions and leaders to respond and solve their problems.[2] In surveying younger "baby busters," George Barna comes to a similar conclusion. In one survey he conducted only one-quarter of baby busters described their "community or government and politics as very important cornerstones of their worldview...Busters tend to view personal investment in community affairs and in politics and government as being of minimal importance."[3]

This basic distrust of politics can translate into apathy and non-involvement as well as greater attention to local issues. The concern to maintain the "purity" (a term often used by the young traditionalists) of their religious traditions and spirituality to the neglect of social concern could be a form of narcissism that shuts out the sufferings of the outside world. Yet, the young adults' participation in their faith communities may also have convinced them that personal involvement is a more effective and tangible agent of change and human betterment than commitment to large-scale, impersonal causes that are far removed from their everyday lives. In a study of evangelicals involved in "megachurches" (large, multi-faceted churches), Donald E. Miller found a mind-set similar to many of the subjects in this book. He found that their "interests were local and particular" rather than based around universal concerns and that they have embraced a "postmodern" worldview. One person Miller interviewed summed up this philosophy with the words, "It's better to visit one person in need than to save all the whales in the world."[4]

The young traditionalists' views on gender roles showed important similarities between the three groups. The Catholics and the Reformed subjects were similar to each other in their support for traditional gender roles. The Reformed subjects were clearly the most "anti-feminist" in their views. They were adamant in their view that homemaking was an important ministry or vocation for women. The Reformed men in particular agreed that women should not exercise leadership positions in society and viewed the recovery of male leadership in home, church, and society as restoring to them a sense of masculinity. The Reformed women were more likely to agree with the Catholic respondents that women can exercise leadership positions in society. Both groups, however, were of the view that wives should be in submission to their husbands and that a women's main responsibility in the family should be to nurture children. The Orthodox subjects were more likely than the others to allow for more flexible male-female roles and to disagree with position that wives should be subservient to husbands.

However, most of the subjects in all three traditions were strongly critical of feminism, especially in its more radical expressions. Even the small minority of women who said they were feminists disassociated themselves from much of organized feminism. They directed their criticisms toward what has been called by Christina Hoff Sommers as "gender feminism." These feminists tend to view male-female relations in terms of a power struggle and claim that most institutions, such as traditional churches, nuclear families, and the state perpetuate male oppression over women. The female subjects would, in varying degrees, be more sympathetic to what Sommers calls "equity feminism," which would call for fairness for women in society, while arguing that such equality does not preclude differences between the sexes (such as in the male priesthood and a greater nurturing role for women in raising families). Sommers notes that many of those critical of gender feminism (which emerged during the 1960s) are late- and post-baby boomers.[5]

Confronting Modernity Through Tradition

All of the young adults' stressed the comprehensiveness of their faiths. They claimed that their adherence to the "whole faith" was an indicator of the seriousness in which they practiced their religions. The Catholic and the Reformed young adults often pointed to the declines experienced by liberal Catholics and mainline and "liberal" evangelical Protestants as ominous signs of what happens when one deviates from the faith. Such a devotion to their tradition provided these young adults with a religious identity that is better able to withstand the tensions and diluting currents of modern life. But in their attempt to find a comprehensive faith, the young traditionalists also share a similarity with their contemporaries on the matter of choice. Sociologist Peter Berger writes that those who have adopted traditional religion today have done so by choice, a "product of the individual's ongoing project of world- and self-construction." Those living within a religious tradition in earlier times saw their faith almost as a genetically given fact that could not be altered. More significantly, Berger argues that a whole range of religious and other lifestyle choices now coexist within an individual's consciousness due to the growing pluralism in society. Today, even in a highly communal or traditionalistic religion, the modern individual still chooses to belong and can choose to leave the group if other options become more attractive.[6]

Writer Johnny Seal refers to the spiritual journeys of today's young adults as being a kind of "confessional mobility". This process of seeking and often switching faiths represents a "sense of collective pilgrimage, the movement from one faith community to another." The growth of religious pluralism and the eroding of denominational boundaries fragments religious loyalties into "niche markets just like magazines, radio stations and TV programming," Seal adds.[7] In listening to accounts of conversions from secular humanism to Buddhism to traditional Catholicism or from being a "Deadhead" (follower of the Grateful Dead) to a conservative Calvinist, I was often struck by how the young adults navigated their religious transitions with disarming ease and agility. In more skeptical moments, I wondered during interviews about what would happen if I revisited the young traditionalists in a few years. Would some have left their adopted faiths and found a new spiritual or ideological home? And, more disturbing, would they defend their new choices in belief or lifestyle with the same tones of certainty and conviction as I heard in the interviews?

The young traditionalists clearly embraced choice and selectivity in the way they retrieved and identified with their traditions. The conservative Reformed teaching of antithesis was called upon far more often than the doctrine of common grace, the transformation of culture, a positive role for the state in providing justice and other themes that have historically found a place in the Reformed tradition. The role of papal authority and discipline, especially as it is expressed in the current papacy of John Paul II, pro-life activism, and hierarchical marriage roles were viewed as more important concerns for the Catholic subjects than the recent emphasis on egalitarian marriage roles by the same pope, the role of the bishops and their teachings on war and peace, the economy, capital punishment, and Catholic social teachings in general. The Eastern Orthodox subjects were more likely to emphasize the spiritual component of Orthodoxy and its impact on their personal well-being often to the exclusion of communal and cultural aspects that have historically also played a part in the faith.

The young traditionalists reinterpreted and selected these elements in their traditions because they are of use in solving particular dilemmas and problems created by modern society. These dilemmas stem from the way modernity has eroded traditional structures that have provided meaning for people throughout history and elevated the role of individual choice.[8] This movement toward choice has created greater fragmentation and privatization in society as a diversity of institutions and value systems, such as the media, emerged that have diluted traditional sources of moral authority and meaning, particularly religious institutions. Such sources of meaning have become increasingly a matter of private choice, thereby weakening the influence of the more public dimensions of religion in creating the mores and community standards of society. The political and economic expansion that has accompanied modernization has created additional side-effects deemed detrimental to society, such as increasing materialism, alienation, and the dehumanization of individuals.

The Reformed young adults were particularly concerned with the way modern life has become fragmented and has lost its sense of wholeness and unity. The Reformed or Calvinistic emphasis on the sovereignty of God over all of life was viewed as the basis for restoring this wholeness to life; if God is sovereign over all of life, then education, politics, science and the arts should all serve Christ and his kingdom. Such a faith compelled them to become more involved and concerned about cultural and political issues. Most of the Reformed subjects supported bringing laws and other institutions into compliance with God's laws. In realizing the difficulty of such a task (especially due to their adherence to the conservative Reformed teaching of antithesis—that Christian and non-Christian worldviews are fundamentally incompatible), the young adults have at the same time sought to create an alternative culture that restores the norms and unity that they feel have been lost or not yet realized in the wider society.

The reassertion of strictly defined gender roles, parental discipline and involvement in their children's education, pro-life activism, creationism, charity work, Sabbath observance, and a strict work ethic are all distinctive marks of such a "Christian worldview." Such a counterculture is viewed by the subjects as a model of what society should look like. The drawback to this conservative Reformed solution to modernity is that its wholistic yet countercultural approach brings its members into sharp conflict with a society based on pluralism and often different values. The expansion of government services into the social sphere (such as in sex education) intensifies such conflict for the Reformed believer, while a decrease in statism might remove such tensions and provide more interaction between this counterculture and the wider society. Although the Reformed see participation in the free market in wholly favorable terms, such economic forces can also assist in the fragmentation of the family and society—the very process the believer seeks to resist. At the same time, however, this strong family-based faith, with its stress on parent-based education and on the vocation of homemaking, has greater resources than more liberal communities in resisting the values and forces of the market.

While the Catholic young adults were also concerned about the fragmentation caused by modernity (as shown by the similar social positions they shared with the Reformed subjects), they tended to focus more on the lack of moral authority in society and in the church. They rebelled not only against doctrinal liberalism but against the elevation of personal autonomy as a positive value in both church and society. The Catholic tradition appealed to them because it provided them with such an authority through its traditions, long history, and clear-cut moral and religious teachings. Adhering to a time-tested set of teachings and rituals, such as the Latin Mass, was more important to their lives as young adults than being part of a close-knit community of faith or building a Christian culture.

The subjects struggled, often against their own Catholic upbringings, to find such a bastion of faith and morality, and they opposed anything or anyone that might dilute it, whether it be the government, the media, dissenting fellow Catholics or "liberal" bishops. As with the Reformed subjects, the Catholics also sought to restore clearer lines of authority within the family. These Catholics' struggle to restore moral and spiritual authority in their lives is complicated by the pluralism and dissent they find within their own church. It is mainly through their religious orders, fellowships, and the Latin Mass that these young adults have been able to rekindle this sense of the power of tradition and authority on a communal level. But it may be more difficult to convince fellow Catholics of the value of such authority when they are living in a society that prizes personal autonomy and rejects the notion that a tradition or church can direct individuals in their life choices.

The Orthodox subjects were more accepting of such effects of modernity as pluralism and privatization than the Reformed and the Catholic young adults. At the same time, the subjects sought spiritual remedies for another set of modern dilemmas through their devotion to the Orthodox liturgy and the practice of the various spiritual disciplines. The Orthodox solution to modernity is not to construct a Christian worldview or counterculture nor to emphasize an external source of moral authority (although, of course, church tradition represents a baseline of authority), but to cultivate a spirituality that would enable the believer to cope with and, in some cases, challenge such problems of modern society as materialism, secularism, and politicization.

The discipline of fasting was viewed by the young adults as a way of putting a limit on materialism and providing a sense of the transcendent in their lives. The liturgy itself represented a zone of sanctity and timelessness in what they see as a mundane and secular world. The Orthodox subjects tended to elevate the spiritual life over social involvement partly because they felt that society and religion was growing increasingly politicized. They often took a neutral or critical stance in the battles over such issues as feminism, gay rights and even abortion because they were viewed as detracting from spirituality and a concern for individuals. The emphasis on the individual and the personal dimension of life found in Orthodox spirituality was valued by the subjects because it helped them resist the growth of such politicization and ideology on both the right and the left. The Orthodox concern for the individual provides a social function in its own right, but it can also prevent these believers from making contributions to society which extend beyond the interpersonal level.

These traditions exact a high cost from their adherents, calling for a high level of devotion and commitment that excludes other religious options, and requires time, financial support, and changes in personal behavior and social lifestyle, but they also provide more benefits than less demanding faiths. This cost/benefit payoff, to borrow economic terminology, could be seen in the case study of Orthodox convert Simeon Bauman. As a Catholic he felt that all the "energy I had invested in the church was not of service to anyone." In Orthodoxy he found a community of like-minded believers who valued the practice of common rituals and thus a "place where I could invest my energy and it wouldn't be wasted." Such an investment yielded to Bauman and other Orthodox young adults not only a vibrant community life but psychological health benefits from Orthodox contemplative and meditative practices.

The Reformed young adults are already reaping the benefits of their faith even when society does not live up to their worldview or standards. They experience a sense of wholeness through their united and "covenant-based" families, their close social network of fellow believers, and their belief that God is in direct control of the world. The cost of adhering to the teachings of the papacy and the Catholic teachings on birth control and marriage paid off for the Catholic young adults as they provided them with a strong sense of religious identity and perhaps even such added benefits (as some claimed) as marital closeness resulting from natural family planning.

Such sociologists as Rodney Stark and Roger Finke argue that those churches with "strict" or demanding religious practices are more likely to grow than more liberal or lax churches that make no demand on their members, since the former groups create commitment and a sense of belonging for their adherents. While maintaining a tension between a religious group and the wider society is often an ingredient in church growth, sociologists also note that too much dissonance between a group and the surrounding culture makes belonging to such a religion too impractical for most people.[9] It is not evident that increasing strict or demanding practices will make the tradition-based groups discussed in this book any more attractive to young adults. The reenactment of timeless rituals and the reaffirmation of ancient and classical Christian creeds and confessions could just as well be greeted with miscomprehension and blank stares from younger generations increasingly shaped by religious individualism and consumerism.

Seeking Tradition In The Spiritual Marketplace

I began this book by asking whether the adoption of traditional religion has anything to do with the consumer approach to spiritual fulfillment pursued by many Americans today. It appears that there is such a connection, as selectivity and choice play a part in how these young adults appropriate their traditions to meet needs in their lives. On another level, being a traditional believer and a spiritual consumer may not represent two different types of religiosity as much as two stages in the cycle of seeking and finding a faith. A spiritual seeker may eventually come across beliefs and practices that are so compelling that he "buys the whole package" and settles down to raise a family in a comprehensive faith. The same man's daughter raised in this cohesive tradition may eventually seek to break out of its cocoon-like embrace and find a more "authentic" faith for herself through sampling the offerings in the spiritual marketplace. Most people do not fall strictly into either the spiritual seeker or traditionalist camps. But it is evident that even many people who are loyal members of a congregation no longer place much stock in theological or denominational identities—a trend that is likely to grow in the years ahead. At this juncture, the 30 young traditionalists depicted in this book do not seem to represent the wave of the future.

And yet, the movements and churches to which these young adults belong seek to preserve and reapply teachings, practices and traditions that have served the social and religious needs of people for centuries. Spiritual seekers and consumers of religion may come to realize that picking and choosing a myriad of beliefs do not provide them with a firm sense of identity, a link with the past and the resources in which to meet their own mortality and other life crises. It is for this reason that individualistic and consumer-based religiosity and tradition may not be total strangers in the future. But it is another question whether many churches can provide such a meeting place between tradition and individual choice and faith.

There are mixed signs about whether mainline denominations are helping its members make such connections with their respective traditions. Although mainline Protestant denominations have historically sought to adapt their traditions to individual experience and belief, such issues as muticultural and gender inclusiveness and other often politicized social concerns continue to receive the most attention by these church leaderships. The concern to minimize doctrinal differences in order to achieve ecumenical unity can also undercut the historical traditions in mainline denominations. Through their "megachurches" and seeker-based services, evangelical churches have found a good deal of success in drawing in disaffected younger generations, but in the process they are increasingly deemphasizing their theological and religious particularities. Catholicism, Eastern Orthodoxy and other tradition-based faiths have a wealth of resources to share, but there remains something of a culture clash between the more individualistic approach of baby boomers and baby busters and these churches (although there are numerous cases of individual congregations that succeed in translating religious traditions to modern believers within all of these traditions).

Writer Laura Nash notes that "traditional religions are failing to link up their own traditions and rituals to the new meaning systems readily apparent in our culture and often exploited in newer forms of religious (or pseudo-religious) expression. [Baby] boomers need help from the church in making these links. Despite their adroitness with symbol and image, they have found that they do not have the power to invent tradition." Nash adds that the "truths of tradition" will most likely reach baby boomers if the churches can break out of their "fixation on old dualistic social issues, such as abortion and the gender of the clergy, and adapt to a more experiential-based worldview based on self-respect and fellowship."[10] Similar difficulty in adopting a tradition may be experienced by the younger baby buster generation which has grown up with a high degree of relativism, especially on religious matters. Researcher George Barna writes that such young people "need the chance to work through the process of arriving at a workable value system, without being chastised for working through the process...In all likelihood, they would appreciate some guidance in their explorations—as long as it is not rigid and self-righteous."[11]

The young adults in this book also expressed a dislike for rigid and "legalistic" approaches to the faith. They frequently criticized leaders and groups that demanded obedience without providing relevant reasons as to why they should follow such teachings. It appears that the parishes, congregations and fellowships mentioned in these pages have made fairly successful attempts to link up with questioning and seeking young adults. It was not a coincidence that most of the young traditionalists were drawn to their faiths through such "seeker-friendly" channels. These organizations are led by those with a special concern to communicate their traditions through language and activities palatable to unchurched and seeking young adults. However, the fact that the Catholic and Reformed subjects made a strong connection between their faith and many political and social issues suggests that these groups' may have difficulty attracting young adults mainly interested in spirituality. It should not be assumed that those who are attracted to traditional Catholicism or the Reformed tradition are necessarily interested in being drafted into the culture wars. Orthodoxy, although less inclined to adapt to contemporary society in its liturgical and organizational structure than the other two traditions, appeared to provide greater breathing space for subjects to "work through" their faith without calling for agreement on divisive social and political issues.

The young traditionalists in this book have demonstrated that traditions can change in order to accommodate new generations, cultures, and ways of life. The contemporary challenge may be for religious traditions to strike up an uneasy truce with individualism and even religious consumerism and the prominent role it plays in the lifestyles of the younger generations. This should not be impossible for traditional believers. As Peter Berger writes:

> It is a traditional, indeed orthodox Christian insight that God works in strange ways. If in the days of old He could work through the Assyrians and equally unappealing agents, it is not unthinkable that He can work today through the social and cognitive structures of the pluralizing consumer culture.[12]

Evangelical writer Johnny Seal views the "confessional mobility" of young adults in their encounter with religious traditions as a way of

> making one's faith one's own. It is an inevitable characteristic of a generation that has been raised in fragmented families, in dislocated neighborhoods, and with little connection to the past. It describes the intentional choices of those who are seeking to follow Jesus in his teachings and practices to put down new roots—to anchor their faith within a larger theological and

ecclesiological   tradition...Thus   serious   discipleship   today necessitates   an   intentional   process   of   confessional authentication.[13]

There is a limit, however, as to how much these traditions can adapt themselves to the spiritual and social needs of modern individuals without losing much of the cohesive and persuasive power which makes them appealing (and ultimately beneficial) to adherents in the first place. For that reason, following in the path of traditional religion will continue to be a difficult endeavor that goes against the stream of a pluralistic consumer society.

ENDNOTES

Introduction

1. Wade Clark Roof, *A Generation of Seekers* (HarperCollins, New York), p. 188.

2. Dean R. Hoge, Benton Johnson and Donald Luidens, *Vanishing Boundaries* (Westminster/John Knox Press, Louisville, 1994), p. 192

3. George Barna, *Baby Busters: The Disillusioned Generation* (Northfield Publising, Chicago, 1994), p. 135

4. Wade Clark Roof in *Yearbook of American and Canadian Churches* (National Council of Churches, New York, 1990), p. 284-294.

5. Barry Kosmin and Seymour Lachman, *One Nation Under God* (Harmony, New York, 1993), p. 249

6. Giles Keppel, *The Revenge of God* (Penn State University Press, 1994), p. 137

7. See the "Indicators" section of *American Enterprise* magazine, November/December, 1995. p. 20. This issue is devoted to American religious conservatives and provides many interesting portraits of traditional believers (both young and old) within Christian, Jewish and Islamic traditions.

8. Lynn Davidman, *Tradition in a Rootless World* (University of California Press, 1991), p. 194

Chapter 1: The Roman Catholic Tradition

1. Roof, *A Generation of Seekers*, p. 232. Also see the summary of Gallup Poll findings on Catholics under the age of 35 in the *New York Times*, April 13, 1996. The article discusses how the young adults in such surveys often speak more about being "good Christians" rather than "good Catholics" and lack a specifically Catholic vocabulary with which to articulate their faith.

2. Patrick McNamara, *Conscience First, Tradition Second* (SUNY Press, Albany, 1992), p. 153.

3. Michele Dillon, "The Persistence of Religious Identity Among College Catholics," in the *Journal for the Scientific Study of Religion*, June, 1996. (Vol. 35, No. 2), p. 168.

4. Andrea Williams, *Generation X Catholics: How Do They Differ From Older Catholics?* (Unpublished paper presented at the conference of the Society for the Scientific Study of Religion, St. Louis, October 27-29, 1995), p. 5

5. This study, by sociologist Dean Hoge, was cited in the "Of Many Things" column by George W. Hunt, S.J., in *America* magazine, March 19-26, 1994, p. 2

6. For an overview of the conservative Catholic press, including many of the newer publications, see the appendix, "Conservative Catholic Periodicals," by John H. Haas in *Being Right: Conservative Catholics in America* (Indiana University Press, Bloomington, 1995), p. 337-344.

7. Patricia Wittberg, *New Religious Communities in Roman Catholicism: Patterns in Ideological Reformulation*, unpublished paper presented at the conference for the Society for the Scientific Study of Religion, Raleigh, N.C., October 29-30, 1994. Wittberg also discusses the rise of new conservative orders in *The Rise And Fall Of Catholic Religious Orders* (State University of New York Press, Albany, 1994), p. 268-271, and in *Pathways To Re-Creating Religious Communities* (Paulist Press, Mahwah, N.J., 1996).

8. Roger Finke, *Growth and Decline in Catholic Religious Orders* (Unpublished paper presented at the conference of the Society for the Scientific Study of Religion, October 27-29, St. Louis, 1995)

9. Andrew Greeley, "Who Are The Catholic 'Conservatives'," in *America*, September 21, 1991, p. 158-162

10. Michael Cuneo, *Catholics Against The Church* (University of Toronto Press, 1989), p. 188

11. See William Dinges's essay on traditionalist Catholicism in *Being Right*, p. 241-269

12. Telephone Interview with Charles Coloumbe, November 24, 1993

13. Telephone Interview with Roger McCaffrey, October 10, 1993

14. Interview With Elizabeth Phelan, September 28, 1993. All subsequent citations of Phelan are from this interview and subsequent telephone interviews.

15. Interview With Mary Hensel, November 23, 1994. Citations to follow are from this interview and subsequent phone interviews.

16. Interview With James Ryan, October 12, 1993. Citations to follow are from this interview and phone interviews.

17. Interview with John Cuvic, October 19, 1993. Cit. to follow are from this interview and phone interviews.

18. Interview with Michael Aubach, May 22, 1994. Cit. to follow are from this interview and phone interviews.

19. Interview with Tara Aubach, May 29, 1994. Cit. to follow are from this interview.

20. Interview with Phillip Holloran, February 19, 1994. Cit. to follow are from this interview.

21. Interview with Scott Eller, June 8, 1994

22. Andrew Greeley, *The Catholic Myth* (Scribner's, New York, 1990), p. 1

23. Interview with Ray Fidelez, Oct. 19, 1993. Cit. to follow are from this interview.

24. Cuneo, *Catholics Against The Church*, Ch. 7

25. Interview with Steven Kramer, September 29, 1993. Cit. to follow are from this interview

26. While it is true that modern Catholic family teachings have upheld both the leadership of the husband and the equality (or "mutual submission") of husband and wife, more recent statments have emphasized the latter, often to the exclusion of headship themes. See the report on the papal document "On The Dignity and Vocation of Women," in *Religion Watch* newsletter, January, 1989. P. 1., and in Richard John Neuhaus' article in *Forum Letter*, December 28, 1988, p. 1

27. One example of such a call for a countercultural Catholic stance can be found in Richard John Neuhaus' article, "To Propose The Truth," in *Crisis* magazine, April, 1994, p. 20-25.

28. See Coulombe's book, *Everyman Today Call Rome* (Charlegmagne Press, Arcadia, Calif., 1987). Jennifer Bradley, "My So-Called Faith," in the *New Republic*, January 9-16, 1995. P. 19-20. For a similar perspective on younger baby boomers and busters and their attitudes on the contemporary church, see Catherine Walsh's "Perspectives" column in *America* magazine, March 25, 1995, p.7

29. Roof, *A Generation of Seekers*, p. 35

Chapter 2: The Reformed Tradition

1. Dean Hoge, Benton Johnson, Donald Luidens, *Vanishing Boundaries* (John Knox/Westminster Press. Louisville, 1994), p. 192

2. Telephone interview with a membership official from the Presbyterian Church in America, April 23, 1994.

3. Telephone interview with Joel Belz, publisher of *World* magazine, December 11 1995.

4. George Marsden in *Reformed Theology in America* (Eerdmans 1987), p. 10

5. Report on Christian Worldview movement in *Religion Watch* newsletter, May, 1989. p. 1-2

6. Interview with Anthony Genelli, November 10, 1993. All citations to follow are from this interview

7. Interview with Bill Wenzel, November 12. All cit. to follow are from this interview

8. Interview with Christine Ishuwa, November 16, 1993. All cit to follow are from this interview.

9. Interview with Tom, Julie Ferre, November 21, 1993. All cit to follow are from this interview

10. Interview with Charles Dornan, February 27, 1994. All cit. to follow are from this interview.

11. Interview with Cynthia Balen, April 10, 1994. All cit. to follow are from this interview.

12. Interview with Sally Michael, November 16, 1993. All cit to follow are from interview

13. Interview with Mark Carbone, November 23, 1993. All cit. to follow are from interview

14. James Davison Hunter, *Evangelicalism: The Coming Generation* (University of Chicago, 1987), p. 162

15. Hunter, p. 163

16. From a *Religion News Service* (February 29, 1996) article on the Alliance of Confessing Evangelicals cited in *Christian News* (March 11, 1996). P. 8. It should be noted that the condemnations of evangelical trends issued by the alliance are also aimed at the Reformed and Lutheran churches themselves. Within these churches there is a growing interest in seeker-based church growth methods that discard traditional styles of worship; several of the largest congregations in the conservative Presbyterian Church in America hold seeker-based services.

17. Interview with Leslie Wenzel, November 12. All cit. to follow are from interview

18. Douglas Wilson, "Embarrassed Men," in *Credenda/Agenda* magazine, Volume 6 Number 1, p. 8

19. Robert Wuthnow, *The Restructuring of American Religion* (Princeton University Press, 1988), p. 319

20. Don and Carol Browning, "Better Family Values," in *Christianity Today*, February 6, 1995, p.32

21. Peter Berger, "Capitalism and the Disorders of Modernity," in *First Things*, January, 1991, p. 15.

Chapter 3: Eastern Orthodoxy

1.Thomas Hopko writing in an editorial in *The Orthodox Church* newspaper, February 1986.

2. Barry Kosmin, Seymour Lachman *One Nation Under God*, (Harmony Books, New York, 1993), p. 290

3. John Garvey, "Eastern Orthodoxy: An Ancient And, To Some, Mysterious Faith Is Enjoying New Vitality In America," in *Atlantic Monthly*, May, 1989, p. 30-37.

4. Telephone interview with Rev. Peter Gillquist, December 13, 1995

5. Julia Duin, "'New' Orthodox Attract Evangelicals," in *Christianity Today*, May 18, 1992, p. 50-51.

6. Telephone interview with the Rev. Angelo Ardimaz of the Young Adult Ministry division of the Greek Orthodox Archdiocese of North and South America, April 12, 1994. There is reported to be a similar phenomenon taking place among ethnic or cradle Orthodox young adults in the Antiochian Orthodox Church.

7. Interview with Mariame Javic; January 30 1994. all citations to follow are from this interview and subsequent telephone interviews

8. Interview with Simeon Baumann, January 27, 1994. All citations to follow are from this interview and subsequent telephone interviews.

9. Interview with Robin Genovese, February 14, 1994. All citations to follow are from this interview and subsequent phone interviews.

10. Interview with Jill Cook, March 10, 1994. All cit. to follow are from this interview and subsequent phone interviews.

11. Interview with Michael Rogoff, January 27, 1994. All cit. to follow are from this interview and subsequent phone interviews.

12. Interview with Wendy Kent, March 10, 1994. All cit. to follow are from this interview.

13. Interview with Susan Miller, February 14, 1994. All cit. to follow are from this interview and subsequent phone interviews.

14. Interview with John Gaglias, April 20, 1994. All cit. to follow are from this interview.

15. Interview with Aileen Koulis, April 29, 1994. All cit. to follow are from this interview.

16. Interview with Peter Rensky, April 8, 1994. All cit to follow are from this interview and subsequent phone interviews.

17. From interview with Ardemaz.

18. H. Paul Chalfont and H.B. Calvacanti, "Collective Life As The Ground Of Implicit Religion," in the journal *Sociology of Religion*, Winter, 1994, p. 452-453.

19. Frank Schaeffer, "The Seduction of Orthodoxy," in the *Christian Activist* newspaper, Vol. 3, 1994, p. 58. I also attended a lecture by Schaeffer

at the St. Paul's Greek Orthodox Cathedral, Hempstead, N.Y., February 25, 1995.

20. Alexander Webster, *The Price of Prophesy: Orthodox Churches on Peace, Freedom and, Security* (Ethics and Public Policy Center, Washington, 1993), p. 20-21.

21. Chalfont and Calvacanti, p. 450-451.

22. Such Orthodox publications as *St. Sophia Quarterly*, *Again*, and the *Christian Activist*, reflect this conservative tendency among converts. An example of this trend is an issue of *Again* (Vol. 17, No. 3) that is devoted to women in the church. The articles affirm the headship of men in the home as well as in the church and offer a general condemnation of most kinds of feminism.

23. Vigen Guroian, "Dancing Alone: Out Of Step With Orthodoxy," in *The Christian Century*, June 7-4, 1995. p. 608-610. For a response to Guroian's charges see the article, "Eleventh- Hour Laborers," by Vincent Rossi in Frank Schaeffer's newspaper, *The Christian Activist*, March 1996, Volume 8, P. 1. Rossi calls for American Orthodox believers to battle modernity in all its forms (including such modern influences as egalitarianism and technology) and is one of the clearest examples of the uniquely countercultural stance of many of the converts (and some cradle Orthodox believers) who are supporting Schaeffer.

Chapter 4: Conclusion

1. From an undated brochure for *Regeneration Quarterly* entitled, "Renew Your Mind; Recall Your Past; Rethink Your World." Another example of such conservative ecumenism is the recent "Evangelical and Catholics Together" statement, where evangelical (including conservative Reformed leaders) and Catholic leaders pledged unity on pro-life and other social concerns and affirmed of a common orthodox Christian faith. The statement is published in the May, 1994 issue of *First Things* magazine. It should be noted, however, that some conservative Reformed leaders have been among the sharpest critics of the "Evangelicals and Catholics Together" statement, claiming that the document undercuts Reformation teachings on justification by faith through grace.

2. Paul C. Light, *Baby Boomers* (W.W. Norton & Company, New York. 1988), p. 158-159

3. George Barna, *Baby Busters: The Disillusioned Generation* (Northfield Publishing, Chicago), p. 61

4. Donald E. Miller, unpublished paper presented at Society for The Scientific Study of Religion, November, 1992, Washington, D.C.

5. Christina Hoff Sommers, *Who Stole Feminism?* (Simon and Schuster, New York, 1994)

6. Peter Berger, *A Far Glory* (Free Press, New York, 1992), p. 45

7. Johnny Seal, "Confessional Mobility: The Search for New Boundaries," in *Regeneration Quarterly*, Spring, 1995, p. 5

8. See Peter Berger's discussion of modernity in *The Heretical Imperative*, (Anchor Press/Doubleday, New York, 1979), Chapter 1

9. See Rodney Stark's and Roger Finke's *The Churching of America* (Rutgers University Press, New Brunswick, 1992) for more on this economic-based analysis of religious commitment, especially pages 250-275. Finke and Stark would argue that the Catholic Church is different from the conservative Reformed and Eastern Orthodox traditions since it has lowered its demands on members (for instance, in personal devotions such as fasting and in deemphasizing traditional teachings). Finke (see endnote 8 in chapter 1) and others have shown that the more conservative Catholic orders and groups have reintroduced "costly" practices and have experienced new growth. But in contrast to more uniformly conservative denominations and traditions, these Catholic groups (except for the separatist traditionalist Catholics) interact within the pluralistic world of wider Catholicism, thus making it more difficult for them to generate a strong sense of identity and community (the cost and rewards) for members.

10. Laura Nash, "Mallway to Heaven? Religious Choice Among the Baby Boomers," in *The Christian Century*, January 5-12, 1994, p. 18

11. George Barna, p. 147

12. Peter Berger, *A Far Glory*, p. 190

13 . Johnny Seal, p. 5

BIBLIOGRAPHY

Books

Appleby, Scott, and Marty, Martin, ed. *Fundamentalisms Observed* (Univ. of Chicago 1991)

Barna, George, *Baby Busters: The Disillusioned Generation* (Northfield Publishing, Chicago, 1994)

Berger, Peter, *A Far Glory* (Free Press, New York, 1992)

Berger, Peter, *The Heretical Imperative* (Anchor Press/Doubleday, New York, 1979)

Coloumbe, Charles, *Everyman Today Call Rome* (Charlemagne Press, Arcadia, Calif., 1987)

Cuneo, Michael, *Catholics Against The Church* (University of Toronto Press, Toronto, 1990)

Davidman, Lynn, *Tradition in a Rootless World* (University of California Press, Berkeley, 1991)

Finke, Roger, and Stark, Rodney, *The Churching Of America* (Rutgers University Press, New Brunswick, 1992)

Greeley, Andrew, *The Catholic Myth* (Scribner's, New York, 1990)

Hoge, Dean; Johnson, Benton; and Luidens, Doonald, *Vanishing Boundaries* (Westminster/John Knox Press, Louisville, 1994)

Hunter, James Davison, 1987, *Evangelicalism: The Coming Generation*, (University of Chicago, 1987)

Jacquet, Constant, ed., *Yearbook of American and Canadian Churches*, (National Council of Churches, 1994)

Keppel, Giles, *The Revenge of God* (Pennsylvania State University Press, University Park, 1994)

Kosmin, Barry and Lachman, Seymour, *One Nation Under God* (Harmony Books, New York, 1993)

Light, Paul C., *Baby Boomers* (W.W. Norton, New York, 1988)

McNamara, Patrick, *Conscience First, Tradition Second* (SUNY Press, Albany, 1992)

Roof, Wade Clark, *A Generation of Seekers* (HarperSanfrancisco, San Francisco, 1993)

Sommers, Christina Hoff, *Who Stole Feminism?* (Simon & Schuster, New York, 1994)

Webster, Alexander, *The Price of Prophesy* (Ethics & Public Policy Center, Washington, 1993)

Weaver, Mary Jo, and Appleby, R. Scott, ed., *Being Right: Conservative Catholics in America* (Indiana University Press, Bloomington, 1995)

Wells, David, ed. *Reformed Theology In America* (Eerdmans, Grand Rapids, 1985)

Wittberg, Patricia, *The Rise and Fall Of Catholic Religious Orders* (State University of New York Press, Albany, 1994)

Wittberg, Patricia, *Pathways To Re-Creating Religious Communities* (Paulist Press, Mahwah, N.J., 1996)

Wuthnow, Robert, *The Restructuring of American Religion* (Princeton Univ. Press, Princeton, 1988)

Periodicals

Again, 1994, Ben Lomand, Calif.

America, 1991, 1994, 1995, New York

American Enterprise, 1995, Washington, D.C.

Atlantic Monthly, 1989, Boston

The Christian Activist, 1994, Mt. Hermon, Calif.

The Christian Century, Chicago, 1994

Christian News, New Haven, Missouri, 1996

Christianity Today, Carol Stream, Il., 1995

Credenda/Agenda, Moscow, Idaho, 1994

Crisis magazine, 1994, Washington, D.C.

First Things magazine, 1991, New York

Forum Letter newsletter, 1988, New York

Journal for the Scientific Study of Religion, 1996, West Lafayette, Indiana

New Republic magazine, 1995, Washington, D.C.

New York Times, 1996, New York

The Orthodox Church newspaper, 1986, Syosset, N.Y.

Regeneration Quarterly magazine, 1995, Princeton, N.J.

Religion Watch newsletter, P.O. Box 652, North Bellmore, NY 11710

Sociology of Religion Journal, 1994, Washington, D.C.

Other Literature

Finke, Roger, *"Growth and Decline in Catholic Religious Orders."* Unpublished paper presented at the conference of the Society for the Scientific Study of Religion, St. Louis, October 27-29, 1995.

Miller, Donald, unpublished paper presented at the Society for the Scientific Study of Religion, Washington, D.C., November, 1992

Williams, Andrea, *"Generation X Catholics: How Do They Differ From Older Catholics?"* Unpublished paper presented at the Society for the Scientific Study of Religion, St. Louis, October 27-29, 1995

Wittberg, Patricia, *"New Religious Communities in Roman Catholicism: Patterns in Ideological Reformulation."* Unpublished paper presented at the Society for the Scientific Study of Religion, Raleigh, N.C., October, 1993.

Brochure for *Regeneration Quarterly* entitled, "Renew Your Mind; Recall Your Past; Rethink Your World." Princeton, N.J. Undated.

Richard P. Cimino is editor and publisher of Religion Watch, a newsletter monitoring trends in contemporary religion. Cimino received an M.A. in Sociology from Fordham University and is also a freelance writer and researcher.